IN SEARCH OF YOUR GERMAN ROOTS

Angus Baxter

In Search of Your German Roots

A COMPLETE GUIDE TO TRACING YOUR ANCESTORS IN THE GERMANIC AREAS OF EUROPE

Fourth Edition, Updated

GENEALOGICAL PUBLISHING COMPANY

Published by Genealogical Publishing Company
3600 Clipper Mill Rd., Suite 260
Baltimore, MD 21211-1953
www.genealogical.com
Library of Congress Catalogue Card Number 2007938206
ISBN 978-0-8063-1784-7
Made in the United States of America

Cover photography by Michael Philip Manheim, courtesy of Folio, Inc.

FOR NAN—my love, my life, my wife

I have not sung for you
One line of all the tribute I would pay
Yet, oh, if you knew
The things that crowd in my head
At the thought of you
Then would you say
"To me belongs
The Song of Songs."

(a poem by Cecil Roberts)

CONTENTS

INTRODUCTION

This book is written to help you trace your ancestors in the "old country"—whether your German forebears came from Germany or Austria or one of the many European countries that had German settlements. It will give you very little information about records on this side of the Atlantic because there are many books available on this subject. Of course, I will talk about major areas of German settlement in North America, such as Pennsylvania and the Midwest, and the Kitchener area of Canada.

Why should you bother to trace your ancestors—those unknown men and women who created you? What benefits will you obtain from your search?

There are no easy answers to these questions but your place in the scheme of things will be more secure. You will know more about yourself and the members of your family who preceded you. When you start to search for your German ancestors you will be setting out on a journey of the heart and mind that will bring you happiness and romance beyond all measure.

No one can say for sure why, all over the world, men and women are searching for their roots. Some, perhaps, hope to find a missing family fortune, some a title of nobility held in abeyance until a claimant comes along, some want to impress their friends with the social standing of great-grandfather, or some to find a family coat of arms. However, I believe the answer is quite a simple one—we, or our children, simply want to know where our family originated and what our ancestors were like.

We want to know what they did, how they earned a living. Why did they leave home to cross the Atlantic? What was happening in their country at that moment in history? What clothes did they wear? What food did they eat? These are our questions and we are the people who will answer them if we are patient and determined.

As you travel back through the years you will acquire no financial rewards—most family stories of missing fortunes are without any foundation—but, on the other hand, you will not have to spend a great deal of money. Of course, you can pay professional researchers to do your work for you, but this is totally unnecessary. Genealogy is a do-it-yourself hobby and this book is designed to help you do just that. Researchers will probably bring you results, but however good they are, they will lack your great personal advantage—your love of your family.

You will need other assets, of course—an organized mind and the patience and determination I mentioned above. You will meet with many obstacles and frustrations. You will meet with difficulties and dead ends. No one ever said ancestor-hunting was easy—or if they did, they didn't know what they were talking about!

You will need to know your history, because the great and remarkable race from which you are so proudly descended has spread across the continent of Europe. Great events of history have changed frontiers, created new countries, destroyed old ones, and through all these cataclysms the German race has left its mark in many areas far beyond the borders of what we now call Germany.

Because you have a German surname and a family story that "great-grandfather came from Germany," do not assume that he came from that area of Europe marked "Germany" on the map. He could have come from Austria, Belgium, the former Czechoslovakia, Denmark, France, Italy, Liechtenstein, Poland, Romania, Switzerland, the former USSR (including the Baltic states of Estonia, Latvia, and Lithuania), or Yugoslavia. All these countries are either German-speaking or have large German minorities. Do not be discouraged. The Germans in these countries kept their own customs, their religion, their ancestral pride, and their records. Their passion for order is a priceless legacy for you.

You can do all your searching by correspondence and exploring the Internet, by working in your own home at your own pace, by using the resources of libraries and archives or church and government records. You do not need to visit the place from which your family came to this country—although one day your own natural curiosity may take you there. Resist the temptation to board a plane tomorrow. You will accomplish much more by sitting down and reading this book—keeping it beside you as you search.

As your work progresses you will be corresponding with people in the old country—priests and ministers, archivists and librarians, friendly civil servants (yes, they do exist!), and genealogical and historical organizations. You will be making contacts and friends—and even distant cousins who will welcome you when you do go overseas. By then, too, you will have learned a great deal about your forebears; you will be able to walk the fields they plowed, worship in the churches they attended, visit the houses in which they lived, and you will not be a stranger in a strange land.

As you turn the pages of this book you will learn about the history of the German people; you will find out how to record the knowledge you will acquire; and you will find out the exact locations of sources of information.

How much will it all cost? How far back will you get? No one can tell you this—it will depend on you and on the state of the records in the area from which your family came. Remember that ancestor-hunting is a pay-as-you-go hobby, and your costs will be spread over a period of time. You, and only you, will control the expenditure. You and only you will decide if you should stop for a while (if you can!) and then start again. Never let this wonderful journey become a drain on your finances.

Don't take on too much research at a time. Start with just one side of your family, otherwise you will only become confused with the dozens of names you will collect as time goes by. "Was that Ernst Müller or Ernst Brand? Was it Anna Frank who came from Munich (München), or was that Anna Fiedler?" You will also find that when you are searching long lists of names it will be much easier to look for one surname than seven or eight. Of course, if two or more sides of your family came from the same village, that is quite a different story—you will save time and money by looking for them simultaneously.

With the passage of time your family tree will grow, and as it does you will find out many things about the people who made you. You will find answers to questions you have often asked, and to questions you have never known you wanted to ask. You may even discover physical appearances and traits of character that will tell you why you are as you are.

As you will read later on in this book, it might help to contact the local newspapers in the old country and ask for information about your family—provided that you know the general area of the country from which they came. Your letter will probably be published if you keep it very short—or it may not. It may bring a response from a sixth cousin—or it may not. You do not know, but in ancestor-hunting you try every possible way to delve into the past. For example, you may be descended from those Germans who settled in Transylvania (then part of Hungary, now in Romania) in the twelfth century. There are still a sufficient number of Germans living in Romania to justify the publication of a weekly newspaper in German. You could try a letter to the editor of *Neuer Weg*, Piata Scinteii 1, Bucharest (Bucuresti), Romania. Who knows what results it will bring?

Finally, you must be warned that in your search, as you go further back in the records, you will be confronted with the old Germanic script. In its printed form it is not too difficult to grasp because it resembles the script used on the title page of many newspapers—the *New York Times*, for example. It is in its handwritten form that the real problems arise. A further complication is that the earlier church records were often written in Latin. I suggest you buy, or try and borrow through your library, an inexpensive booklet, *If I Can You Can Decipher Germanic Records,* by Edna M. Bentz. It was privately published in San Diego in 1982 (reprint 2006). It is the most helpful book I know because it not only explains and illustrates Germanic script, but also lists handwritten examples of many of the words you will encounter in your own research—emigrant, sponsor, sergeant, innkeeper, lessee, miner, farmer, priest, settler, and so on.

Enough of these preliminary words of wisdom! With the aid of this book you are starting on an exciting voyage, and no one knows where it will take you or what treasures you will find along the way. Perhaps there really was a castle on the Rhine once owned by your family—maybe an ancestor stood on the battlements of Marksburg and watched the ships sail slowly by on the river far below. All this lies ahead with the discoveries you will make as you search for your German roots.

It is much easier now than when this book was originally written to search for your German ancestors, thanks to the Internet. All of the major archives and many of the smaller ones and church parishes have websites containing contact information and information on their holdings. Correspondence can now often be handled more quickly and less expensively via e-mail. An ever increasing number of databases with information relevant to German ancestor-hunters—passenger lists, cemetery records, surname directories, etc.—has greatly improved opportunities for research. While these developments in no way alter the nature of the records or the research techniques described in this work, readers should be aware that the growing list of websites, online databases, and CD-ROMs devoted to German genealogy have made the task of locating your German ancestors immeasurably easier. This edition of the book includes website and e-mail addresses whenever possible, and lists numerous online resources that will be invaluable in your search. Be aware, however, that URLs and e-mail addresses change frequently. If you find a URL or address that is no longer accurate, do an Internet search for that organization to locate its new URL.

I have been helped by many kindly and co-operative people who provided me with information about genealogical sources. There are too many people to mention all of them, but there are some I must thank by name:

Thomas Schmid, First Secretary, German Embassy, Ottawa

Fr. Regina Mittner, German Embassy, Ottawa

Dr. Udo Hahn, Oberkirchenrat, Vereinigte, Evangelical-Lutheran Church, Hannover

Dr. Peter Vorster, Direktor, Herder-Marburg Institute

Dr. H. Wentner, German Bishops' Conference, Catholic Church, Bonn

Telephone Numbers

The international telephone and fax numbers that appear in this book have been presented in such a way that readers may call from the United States.

Starting the Search

Start with you and with no one else. Do not take someone with your surname who was famous two centuries ago and try and trace his or her descendants down to you. First, it is impossible and, second, there is little likelihood of a family connection anyway. Names can be misleading in four ways:

1. Even within a few generations of a family the spelling of a name can change. Usually this was because, with a few exceptions, our ancestors could not read and write and so the name would be spelled phonetically (as it sounded). There was, in fact, a double complication, for the name could sound different to different people. Just as some people are tone-deaf to music, so other people are word-deaf. The spelling changes could occur on different occasions—when your ancestor was arranging with the local clergyman for a baptism, a marriage, or a burial; when he was registering with the local police for an internal passport; when he was answering the questions of the census enumerator; when he was registering for compulsory military service; when he was booking passage on a ship; or even when a name was being carved on a tombstone. In my own family records you will find Baxter, Backster, Bagster, Bacaster, Bacster, Bakster, Bacchuster—even Bastar (I didn't like that one very much!). In Germany, for example, Meyer can be spelled as Mayer, Meier, Meir, Mier, or Maier.

2. Don't assume that everyone with the same name as yours must be related to you somewhere back in time. Up until the fourteenth century (and much later in some parts of Europe) there were no surnames. People were known by their first name, and attached to it was a word describing where they lived or what they did, or even an event such as a flood that took place when they were born. So a man named Wilhelm might be Wilhelm from the wood (Wald), or Wilhelm the baker (Bäcker), or Wilhelm the wagonmaker (Wagner), or Wilhelm born in the storm (Sturm). Sometimes, too, a newcomer to a village would be known, for example, as Wilhelm from Erlangen (this would be written

as Wilhelm von Erlangen, so I am sorry to say a "von" in your ancestral name does not necessarily mean your forebears were noblemen!). By about 1400 the population growth and increasing movement of the population made the lack of a surname a nuisance and so the "the" or "of" or "from" was dropped.

3. You may find your surname was changed a couple of generations back. This could happen for several reasons—your ancestor may have decided his name was too long or too complicated for use in a new country and so he might have made it shorter; or he may have decided to anglicize his name so that Schmidt became Smith; or he might have encountered some bigot of an immigration officer who said, "Rosenkrantz? What sort of name is that? I'll put you down as Rose."

4. In certain areas, particularly in Holstein and Ostfriesland, the system of patronymics was used (giving children a surname based on their father's first name), so that Peter Bergmann could have a son with the name of Wilhelm Peters. In some cases, too, a man might have a surname based on the name of his farm, and if he moved to another farm his surname would change. However, patronymics and farm names are not always a problem because usually the real family name was entered afterwards in parentheses as "sonst" (meaning otherwise) or "angenommener" (meaning adopted).

Make a list of all known living members of your family, including even the most distant cousins, with their addresses. Then add to the list the names and addresses of old family friends if they are known to you.

Once this is done you can start to ask questions—in person, on the phone, and by mail or e-mail. Write down everything you are told and be sure you also write down the name of the person who gave you the information—you may need to query an item with that person later on.

If by any chance you have elderly relatives, this may be like striking the mother lode. They might well know when and where people were born or died, who married whom and, in some cases, who *had* to marry whom! Remember, too, that they can tell you not only about the events of their own lives, but also about events they heard of from their grandparents. In the clear mind of an elderly person you may find 150 years of family history—a rich source of material just waiting to be uncovered.

When you are about to approach great-aunt Erika for help, please take care—particularly if you do not know her all that well and rarely visit her. Do not arrive unannounced with a tape recorder and a long list of prepared questions that you fire at her with military precision. If you do this you will get very little. Older people do not like tape recorders, and their minds, though quite clear, do not react instantly to a barrage of questions. Always make an appointment, explain what you are doing, tell them you will be grateful if they will share their knowledge and wisdom with you, and then go and see them with a small notebook, plus a supply of charm and patience. Then just sit and chat away like old friends, take notes quietly and unobtrusively, and you will learn a lot. Don't overtire them, and when you leave, say, "I would like to talk to you again. You have told me so many fascinating things. I want to come and see you again, and perhaps in the meantime you could jot down a note about any other things you remember." I guarantee that you will learn much more at the second visit than you do at the first! Of course, you will hear a lot of stories that are not of direct value to you, but if you have any sense of history you will benefit from these as well.

If you do have this elderly relative in your family, talk to him or her now—don't delay, don't put off going to see them. Almost every ancestor-hunter will say to you, "If only I had talked to my great-aunt and listened to her stories when she was alive. Now she is dead, and all her knowledge of the family went with her."

Ask everyone about everything you need to know—date of arrival in this country, name of the ship, port of arrival, occupation, religion, place of origin, place of death, place of burial, military service, date of naturalization—some of this information you will have already, some you will need to search hard for, but it will all help you along the road. So far as religion is concerned, a word of caution: coming from Germany, your family will probably be either Catholic or Evangelical Lutheran. Remember that people can change their religion—either through marriage, conversion, or happenstance. The latter could occur if your deeply religious ancestor settled in a place in this country where there was no Lutheran church. There might have been a Methodist chapel, and so he might have decided to attend services there. When a Lutheran church was built he would have reverted to his original denomination, but for a period of several years the vital events of the family may have been recorded in the Methodist church registers.

I mentioned earlier the importance of talking to *every* member of your family. Just one member may have information unknown to anyone else. Let me tell you a story.

My wife was born in Scotland and so were her parents and grand-parents and several generations beyond them. When she was a small child her grandfather mentioned to her that the family had come from England 200 years before. She remembered this, and many years later she commented about the story to her father. He told her there could not be any truth in it—the family was Scots way back forever (you must understand that if you are Scots and have English blood in your veins you keep quiet about it!).

When we started to trace my wife's family back we remembered grandfather's story and, without going into all the details, we found he was right to within twenty years. What is more, we traced the man who came from England and found a published family tree in a history book, which took us back to 1680 and gave us clues that eventually took us back to 1296. All because one member of a family was told something vital.

So some family stories are true, but many are not, and all stories should be treated with caution until you have proof as to their truth. I am not suggesting you are descended from Baron von Münchhausen but, let's be honest, over the years a certain amount of decoration can creep in. You may have been told about the Rhine castle I mentioned, but perhaps your ancestors only worked there, or were tenant farmers on the estate. You may have been told that great-grandfather was an officer in the Prussian army at the Battle of Sedan in 1870, whereas he was really a Feldwebel or sergeant.

When you start talking to members of your family you may meet with resistance from one or two who may say, "Leave well enough alone," "Let sleeping dogs lie," "Don't stir the pot, you don't know what will come to the top," and so on and so on. Try and overcome this sort of hindrance. They are probably afraid you will discover something to the discredit of the family, some rogue who stole a sheep, some skeleton in the closet. Maybe—horror of horrors!—great-grandfather was illegitimate. Who cares! Anyway, if it bothers you at all, remember you are not publishing your family tree in the local newspaper. It is very unlikely you will discover a bastard in your ancestry. So far as resistance is concerned, you must use all your well-known charm and tact—explain that even if there is something in the family background, you promise to say nothing about it to anyone else.

There is one other important thing you must never forget. You can send simple queries by e-mail but may have to depend on "snail mail" if you are requesting more detailed information or anticipate receiving papers that can't be sent to you electronically. Be sure you always send return postage when you write to anyone for information—even government departments overseas. If you do not, you may not get an answer. Remember you are not the only person writing for information. Tens of thousands of people are tracing their ancestors and writing letters, and most of them do not cover the cost of the return postage, so now the general rule has become "no postage no answer." You can do this by buying three International Reply Coupons (IRCs) from your local post office (or as many IRCs as are needed to cover return postage—you can e-mail first to find out how many are needed) and enclosing them with your letter. You should also enclose a No. 10 self-addressed envelope. The recipient can exchange the IRC coupons for stamps at the local post office. There is also another way to do it. If you know you will be settling down to quite a lot of correspondence with, let us say, Austria, then you can get a draft for ten dollars from your bank, mail it to the Direktor, Postamt, Vienna (Wien), Austria, with a letter saying, "I enclose a draft for ten dollars. Please send me the equivalent value in Austrian stamps of the correct denomination for airmail postage to this country." This will save you about 40 percent of the cost compared with coupons.

When you are writing to archives, genealogical organizations, clergymen, officials of all kinds, remember they are not compelled to answer you. There is no international law that says they must. So be sure to write a nice, polite letter, give them as much background as you can about the subject of your inquiry, but make it brief and to the point, and thank them in advance for their kind assistance. The words "mit freundlichen Grüssen" before you sign your name can unlock many doors!

Quite apart from talking and writing to family members and friends, you must also search for family records of all kinds—letters, diaries, naturalization papers, family Bibles, family photograph albums, etc. A word of warning, though, about family Bibles. It was fashionable up until about 1900 to present one to a newly married couple so they could record the vital events of the new family—births and baptisms, and, eventually, marriages and deaths and burials. Special pages were provided for such records, either at the front of the Bible or between the Old and New Testaments. Often, people starting to trace their ancestors accept all the handwritten entries as "gospel," but "it ain't necessarily so," as Gershwin put it. If all the entries are in the same handwriting with no variation in style and neatness over more than two generations, the odds are that many entries were made long *after* the event and are, therefore, based on "hearsay" and are not reliable without other confirmation.

The family photograph album you possess is probably the most frustrating record you will find. There are all those lovely pictures of solemn-looking men and women who must be ancestors—but, unfortunately, no one has written their names below the photograph or on the back. Possibly your elderly relative can help to identify some of them for you. However, there is one clue in the album that may be of value to you. The chances are that the name and city of the photographer of any studio pictures will be printed or embossed on the front or back of them. If this same city is repeated several times, it is quite likely to be the place from which your immigrant ancestor came. He may have brought some of the photos with him, or they may have been sent out by the family he left behind—"Here is a photograph of your brother

Heinrich and his new wife, Elisabeth." You can also use this clue of a possible place of origin in two other ways, both of which you are going to use anyway—first, to check if someone has already traced your family and, second, to try to find relatives still living in Europe.

This is what you must do:

1. *Has someone already traced your family back?* There are a number of databases available on the Internet containing information on millions of surnames. You can find many of these listed at **www.cyndislist. com,** type your surname into a search engine, or visit two of the largest genealogical communities on the Internet—**Ancestry.com** (Ancestry.de for the German version) and **Rootsweb.com.** You can also check out the following organizations to see if they have any record of the family:

    (a) Visit the website of The Church of Jesus Christ of Latter-day Saints (the LDS Church) at **www.familysearch.org** or visit one of their branches. The church requires that its members trace their ancestors and, as a result, holds the largest collection of genealogical material in the world. This is described in detail later in this book.

    (b) Write to (or visit) the public library of the place in this country where your ancestor settled, and the library in the place from which he came (or you think he came). Write also to national, provincial, and local archives in the particular area in Europe. Get in touch with genealogical societies and family history societies in the same area.

        In all these cases explain what you are doing and give as much information as you can about the sailing date, date of arrival in this country, place of settlement, religion, and occupation.

        So far as local archives are concerned you should also give the name of the photographer named in your album and ask if he is still in business or, if he is not, whether his office records and original photographic plates have been given to the archives (this does happen occasionally and is worth inquiring about since you are writing anyway).

2. *How do you find out if you have living relatives in Europe?* Of course, you try to find this out from within your own family, but if you fail to discover anything, then there are two methods to use:

    (a) If you know or believe your ancestor came from a particular small city or town or village, send an e-mail or write a brief letter to the local newspaper. If your ancestor came from a big city like Berlin, Munich, or Vienna, the big dailies are unlikely to publish it—small-town or county papers will nearly always do so.

If you don't know the name of the local newspaper, it doesn't matter. Try an Internet search or simply write to Der Redakteur, Die Zeitung, Nürnberg (or whatever is the name of the town or area in which you are interested). Your letter should be short and on the following lines:

> My grandfather, Alois Furst, emigrated from your area in 1890. He was a farm worker. His father was named Johann. If there are any relatives still living in Nürnberg I would very much like to hear from them.

At this point you may be saying, "My grandfather emigrated a century ago—even if he left brothers and sisters behind, there will be no one alive to know about him." You are wrong! Do you realize that when grandfather emigrated this was the most shattering event ever to occur in his family? A son, a brother, was leaving home to cross the ocean to the other side of the world, never to be seen again. The event was, and is, unforgettable, and whenever this country is in the news someone over there will be saying, "Of course, grandfather had a brother who emigrated. We must have lots of cousins over there." They won't take any initiative to find *you*, but a letter to the local paper may help you find *them*!

(b) Another possible source of information is the telephone directory. Many international telephone directories are now available online. For example, complete German telephone directories—with numbers for archives, individuals, and businesses—are available at **http://members.cox.net/hessen/ telephones.htm#telefonbuch** and **http://www4.dastelefon buch.de/**. If you have an uncommon German name, you can write to the embassy or nearest consulate of Germany, or whichever country is involved, and ask if they would be kind enough to photocopy the page in the local phone book for the place or area in which you are interested. If your name is Muller forget it! If it is Klippenhoffer then try it! The name must be uncommon, otherwise the method is not practical. Once you have your list of names and addresses—hopefully about twenty or thirty—then you can send a letter to the first five. If it brings no results then write to the next five, and so on. Be sure to include your e-mail address so that people can reply to you that way. Here again, be brief and say:

> I saw your name in the phone book. My grandfather, Alois Furst, emigrated from your area in 1890. His father was named Johann. If you are descended from his brothers or sisters, or are in any way related to him, I would very much like to hear from you.

This is as good a place as any to talk about language. Of course, it is better if you can write all your letters of inquiry in German—to archives, to libraries, to churches, to newspapers, and to names in a phone book. However, if you have lost your ancestral language, try and get your letters translated by a family friend who speaks the language, by a local high school teacher, or by the local German society or organization. If all else fails, it is better to write in good English than in bad German.

You will probably get responses from people who are not related but are complete strangers going out of their way to help you. People all over the world are, generally speaking, kind and friendly—it is the other kind, unfortunately, who hit the headlines! Let me give you an example of what may happen to you—it happened to me.

My family originated in a remote valley in the Lake District of England. I traced them back in a proven and continuous line to 1340, and from then with gaps to 1195. Several years ago I wrote a letter to the *Westmorland Gazette* (the local paper) asking if, by any chance, a reader had photographs of the houses and farms in which my ancestors had lived (I listed them) and, if so, could they lend me prints to be copied, or have them copied in England at my expense.

I had three replies from people who did not have any photographs but who had made special journeys to the valley to photograph the houses for me. One couple even made a fifty-foot movie of the valley for me. So try letters to newspapers.

Now, one final word of advice before we move on to German history. I mentioned above that you should contact family history societies for information as to whether anyone has already traced, or is tracing, your family. You should also give some thought to becoming a member of the organization covering the district from whence your ancestors came, providing that you are not experiencing language problems. There are several good reasons for joining such a society:

1. It publishes a newsletter at regular intervals and you will obtain a great deal of information about the area and its genealogical records.

2. It will keep you up-to-date as to new sources of information, and old ones that have just reappeared after many missing years.

3. It will publish your queries in the newsletter free of charge.

4. It lists the names and addresses of members and the names for which they are searching.

If you are interested in Germans from the Palatinate there is a society, and if you are interested in Germans from Prussia there is a society for that area too. Many of these are listed later on in this book.

There were important changes in the German Postal Code system after the unification of East and West Germany. Before unification the postal codes for each location had the prefix O or W to distinguish between

East and West Germany. All numbers were four-digit. Now there is a five-digit code applicable to the whole country. It is very important that you use the postal code because of the duplication of place-names in the country. There are, for example, a dozen places named Königsberg! Some of them are tiny villages.

The Germans and Germany

If we think about our German ancestry, it is easy to be led astray by lack of knowledge of the original Germanic tribes and their descendants. Without this knowledge it is difficult to avoid making mistakes that may delay or even halt forever our search for our German roots.

When we read about German colonies we only find mention of Tanganyika, Southwest Africa, the Cameroons, and Western Samoa, but over many centuries the hardy and adventurous German race has, in fact, colonized many parts of Europe.

A number of different tribes formed the German race more than a thousand years ago—Franks, Bavarians, Saxons, and Swabians, to mention only a few of them. Today, German is the mother tongue of 100 million people.

The development and coalescence of the German nation took many centuries. The word "Deutsch" (German) was first used in the eighth century, but it only referred to the spoken language of the area known as eastern Franconia. This empire reached its height of importance under the Emperor Charlemagne (Karl der Grosse), and after his death in 814 it disintegrated. The western section eventually became the area we now know as France. The eastern section varied in area over the centuries, but the main area—the heartland—became known as the Deutschland (the land of the Germans). By 911 the Duke of Franconia was elected King of the Franks, and later King of the Romans. By the eleventh century the area became known as the Roman Empire, and by the thirteenth the Holy Roman Empire. In the fifteenth century the words "German Nation" were added.

Before and during all these dynastic and political events, the German tribes overran most of the original Roman Empire as far east as the Elbe—beyond it were the fierce Slavic tribes. During this period the tribes took firm root in what we now know as Switzerland, Liechtenstein, Austria, northern Italy, the Netherlands, and the Baltic states. They were also invited into Transylvania by the Hungarian king in 1150.

Siebenburgen—the German name for Transylvania—derives from the seven fortified towns established by the Germans. Although they came from the Rhine and Moselle area, they were known as "Saxons." There were some 5,000 settlers who were given as much land as they could cultivate and allowed to retain their own customs and language. Some did not stay long but moved south into the area known as the Banat, or west into Hungary proper. After eight centuries their descendants are still in Transylvania. However, there are now only some half-million of them, since the rest fled to Germany when the Communists took over after the Second World War.

While all this was going on, the Order of the Teutonic Knights and the Livonian Brothers of the Sword were extending German power into the Baltic countries of Estonia, Latvia, and Lithuania. The Teutonic Knights were formed originally to take part in the Crusades, but eventually settled in Prussia in 1309 , and then extended their power and influence eastward into Livonia and Courland. At the same time King Andrew II of Hungary called on the Teutonic Knights to protect Transylvania from the Cumans and the Mongols in the east. So both northeastern and southeastern Europe were "colonized" by the Germans. The prime aim of the Knights was conquest and loot, but behind them came settlers, bringing a predominant German influence into the conquered territories. The Drive to the East (Drang nach Osten) started with Charlemagne's armies and the Teutonic Knights, and ended with Hitler.

During this period there were also smaller migrations to Schlesien (Silesia), which is now divided between the Czech Republic and Poland, and to Bessarabia—until 1945 Romanian and now largely in Moldova. In the reign of the empress Maria Theresa of Austria (1740–1780) many Germans—the so-called Danubian Swabians—migrated to four areas of Hungary: Bacska, the Banat, the Kingdom of Croatia, and part of Slovakia. A number of these settlers later moved on into Ukraine, Bessarabia, and other areas of southern Russia. Others—like the Zipsers—settled in Slovakia.

After the First Partition of Poland in 1772, Frederick the Great of Prussia (1740–1786) settled West Prussia and the area around Bromberg with German immigrants from Württemberg and Baden-Durlach. Said the king, "Get me farmers from Württemberg and the economic misery will come to an end."

In the middle of the eighteenth century the empress Catherine the Great of Russia (1762–1796) invited all foreigners who possessed skills of some kind to come to her country as settlers and colonists. In cases of financial hardship the cost of transportation was paid. In addition, all settlers received a loan of money toward the cost of building a house and buying livestock and farm or trade equipment—with repayment required in ten years.

The proclamation of the empress was distributed throughout Europe but did not meet with any great response except in the Germanic area and, to a much smaller degree, Sweden. Most of the colonists came from Hesse (Hessen) and the Rhineland, but all German-speaking areas were represented in varying numbers.

I must quote to you the titles of the empress as set out in her proclamation. No, it will not help your genealogical research one little bit, but I found it amusing and so, I hope, will you:

> Empress and Autocrat of all the Russians at Moscow, Kiev, Vladimir, Novgorod, Czarina of Kazan, Czarina of Astrachan, Czarina of Siberia, Lady of Plaskow, Grand Duchess of Smolensko, Duchess of Estonia and Livland, Carelia, Twer, Yogoria, Permia, Viatka, and Bulgaria and others; Lady and Grand Duchess of Novgorod in the Netherland of Chernigov, Resan, Rostov, Yaroslav, Belooseria, Udoria, Obdoria, Condonia, and Ruler of the entire North Region and Lady of the Yurish, of the Cartalinian and Grusinian czars, and the Cabardinian land, of the Cherkessian and Gorisian princes, and the lady of the manor and sovereign of many others.

The areas opened up for settlement by the empress were underpopulated and open to frequent attacks by the Ottoman Turks. The Germans, for their part, were eager to settle for a variety of reasons. Germany as we know it today did not exist. It was a vast conglomeration of 1789 kingdoms, principalities, grand duchies, dukedoms, electorates, free states, and free cities—down to tiny independent states of a few hectares. Men were dragged off into various warring armies, women and children were raped or killed or both, agriculture was ruined by the constant wars, and people starved. There was also religious persecution, high taxes, civil disturbances, and in many areas a high population density. Life was miserable and dangerous for the ordinary people, and it was no wonder the grass in the next field looked much greener.

If your family is descended from the Germans who emigrated to Russia between the mid-1700s and the mid-1800s, you may have assumed there is no chance of tracing your forebears back to their place of origin in the area that is now Germany. In fact, there is a very good chance records exist that will give you vital information.

Between 1804 and 1842 over 72,000 people emigrated to Russia, and estimates for the entire period range as high as 150,000 from the German area alone. It was one of the great mass movements of history. For a century they poured into Russia and established themselves in fairly close areas of settlement in the Volga region, the Black Sea area, and the Caucasus.

The whole story is documented in a remarkable two-volume work by a very remarkable man—Dr. Karl Stumpp. It is entitled *The Emigration from Germany to Russia 1763–1862* and was published by the

American Historical Society of Germans from Russia (AHSGR), 631 D Street, Lincoln, NE 68502 (phone: 402-474-3363; e-mail: ahsgr@ ahsgr.org; website: www.ahsgr.org). It lists the names of some 50,000 German settlers, with their places of origin and settlement. The AHSGR also maintains a website at **www.ahsgrsoar.org** called "Saving Our Ancestral Records" (SOAR), where you can access obituaries, census and cemetery records, family group cards, maps, newspapers, photos, reference books, surname charts, passenger lists, Bessarabian vital records, AHSGR publications, and more. Information is available for persons from multiple German Russian regions.

It may be helpful to quote the areas of origin and settlement over the century:

Period of Emigration	Place of Origin	Area of Settlement
1763–68	Hessen, Rheinland, Pfalz, Sachsen, Württemberg, Switzerland	Volga (E and L)
1765	Sulzfeld, Württemberg	Reibensdorf (E)
1766	Hessen, Württemberg, Brandenburg	Petersburg, Black Sea
1766	Hessen	Belowesh (E and C)
1780	Preussen, Württemberg, Bayern	Josefstal, Fischerdorf, Jamburg, in Dnieper area
1782	Sweden	Schwedendorf (E)
1786	Preussen	Alt-Danzig
1789–90	Danzig, West Preussen	Chortitza (M)
1804–6	Alsace, Pfalz, Baden	Franzfeld, Mariental, Josefstal, by Odessa (C)
1804–6	Württemberg, Alsace, Pfalz, Baden, Hungary	Grossliebental, Neuburg, Alexanderhilf
1804–6	Danzig, West Preussen	Halbstadt, Molotschna (M)
1804–6	Württemberg, Baden, Hessen	Prischib, Molotschna (E and C)
1804–6	Württemberg, Switzerland	Neusatz, Zürichtal, in the Crimea (E and C)
1808–10	Württemberg, Alsace, Pfalz	Bergdorf, Glückstal, Kassel, Neudorf, by Odessa (E)
1808–10	Alsace, Baden, Poland	Baden, Elsass, Kandel, Selz, Mannheim, Strassburg (C)
1808–10	Alsace, Baden, Pfalz, Württemberg	Beresan and Odessa (C)
1812–27	Württemberg, Baden, Hessen	Prischib, Molotschna (E)
1814–16	Württemberg, Preussen, Bayern, and Poland	Bessarabia, and near Odessa
1817–18	Württemberg	South Caucasus (E)
1821–34	Württemberg, Preussen, Bayern, and Poland	Bessarabia, and near Odessa

Period of Emigration	Place of Origin	Area of Settlement
1822–31	Württemberg	Swabian colonies near Berdjansk (E)
1823–42	Danzig, West Preussen, Baden, Hessen, Rheinland	Grunau area (E and C)
1853 and 1859–62	Danzig, West Preussen (This was the last emigration from Germany)	Samara (M)

(E=Evangelical, L=Lutheran, C=Catholic, M=Mennonite)

When the German armies invaded the USSR in 1941 they were welcomed by the majority of the Germans living in Ukraine. When the Wehrmacht retreated in 1942 many of the German settlers left too, fearing reprisals from the Red Army, and they were wise. They made their way back to Germany, the fatherland their ancestors had left more than a century before, and those left behind in Ukraine were killed or imprisoned.

Millions of Germans in other areas of Europe became refugees after the Second World War. In 1945 Czechoslovakia regained the Sudetenland. This German-speaking area had been taken from Austria in 1919. In 1938 it was reunited with Germany. After 1945 the three-and-a-half million German inhabitants were expelled and their property and possessions confiscated. Other refugees from Poland and the USSR brought the total number of Germans returning home to over thirteen million.

Quite apart from the mass movements of population shown above, there was, of course, a continual movement to and fro between the multitude of German states before and after unification in 1871. Most of these movements of individuals were recorded, and the records are in the various state archives. If a man wished to move from Hannover to Brunswick, for example, he would notify the Hannover police of his impending departure and his destination. On arrival in Brunswick he had to report to the police within three days. They, in turn, notified the Hannover police that he had arrived.

Although these tremendous upheavals will have a major effect on your ancestor-hunting, you must also become aware of other problems ahead. For example, there are large numbers of Germans still in Denmark, Belgium, and Alsace (Elsass), and many German speakers in the South Tirol—now in Italy.

In addition, you must consider the "lost territories" of Germany and what has happened to their genealogical records. These territories consist of the following areas:

To Belgium: In 1919 Eupen, Malmédy, and Moresnet
To Czechoslovakia: In 1945 the western part of Silesia (Schlesien)
To Denmark: In 1920 North Schleswig

To France: In 1919 Alsace (Elsass)
To Poland: In 1945 the eastern parts of Brandenburg, Pomerania (Pommern), the southern part of East Prussia (Ostpreussen), Posen, the western part of Silesia (Schlesien), West Prussia (Westpreussen), and Danzig
To the USSR: In 1945 the northern part of East Prussia (Ostpreussen) and Memel

The genealogical records for these areas are located in the various archives listed below:

Belgium: Church and civil records of the transferred area are in the State Archives at Liège (Archives de l'État à Liège, Rue du chéra 79, 4000 Liège; e-mail: Archives.Liege@arch.be; website: http://arch.arch.be/).

Czech Republic: The two major cities from Silesia now in this country are Leitmeritz (now Litoměřice) and Troppau (now Opava). The addresses of the two archives are:

Státní oblastní archiv
Dominikánsky Kláster
Krajská 1, 41274 Litoměřice
Phone: 011-420-477-755971. Fax: 011-420-477-755992
E-mail: info@soalitomerice.cz
Website: www.soalitomerice.cz/

Zemský archiv v Opavě
Sněmovní 1
746 22 Opava
Phone: 011-420-553-607240. Fax: 011-420-553-607247
E-mail: podatelna@zao.archives.cz
Website: www.archives.cz/

Denmark: The old Duchy of Schleswig-Holstein was divided in 1920. The northern part went to Denmark and the southern part remained German. Records for the latter part are in the Landesarchiv Schleswig-Holstein (Prinzenpalais, D-24837 Schleswig, Germany; e-mail: landesarchiv@la.landsh.de; website: www.landesarchiv.schleswig-holstein.de/). The census records for the area lost by Germany are located in the Landsarkivet for Sønderjylland (Haderslevvej 45, 6200 Aabenraa, Denmark; e-mail: mailbox@laa.sa.dk; website: www.sa.dk/laa/). The church records for the northern part are also in these archives, as are copies of some of the Holstein records.

France: For information regarding Alsace-Lorraine contact the following archives:

Archives départementales du Bas-Rhin
5 rue Fischart
67000 Strasbourg
E-mail: archives67@cg67.fr
Website: www.archives.cg67.fr/

Archives départementales du Haut-Rhin
Cité administrative
3, rue Fleischhauer
68026 Colmar Cedex
E-mail: archives@cg68.fr
Website: www.archives.cg68.fr/

Archives départementales du Moselle
1, allée du Château
57076 Metz Cedex 3
Website: www.archives57.com/

Minitel in France maintains a searchable index (www.genealogy.tm.fr/acte.htm) of online vital records from the Alsace-Lorraine area for the period 1539-1907.

Poland: The country is divided into counties (voivods) and each has its own archives. Those of the following cities and the area around them are in these various archives. The original German name is given first and then the new Polish name and postal code are in parentheses. Mail inquiries should be sent to Archiwum Państwowe, followed by the postal code and the city or town name in Polish:

Allenstein (10-520 Olsztyn); e-mail: sekretariat@olsztyn.ap.gov.pl; website: www.olsztyn.ap.gov.pl/

Breslau (50-215 Wrocław); e-mail: wroclaw@ap.wroc.pl; website: www.ap.wroc.pl/

Bromberg (85-009 Bydgoszcz); e-mail: info@archiwum.bydgoszcz.pl; website: www.bydgoszcz.ap.gov.pl/

Danzig (80-958 Gdańsk); e-mail: apgda@gdansk.ap.gov.pl; website: www.gdansk.ap.gov.pl/

Grünberg (66-002 Zielona Góra); e-mail: archiwzg@poczta.onet.pl; website: www.archiwum.zgora.pl/

Kattowitz (40-145 Katowice); e-mail: kancelaria@katowice.ap.gov.pl; website: http://katowice.ap.gov.pl/

Köslin (75-950 Koszalin); e-mail: secretariat@koszalin.ap.gov.pl; website: www.koszalin.ap.gov.pl/

Oppeln (45-018 Opole); website: www.archiwum.opole.pl/

Pless (43-200 Pszczyna) (branch of the Katowice archives); e-mail: appszczyna@katowice.ap.gov.pl; website: www.katowice.ap.gov.pl/ang/en_pszcz.html

Posen (60-967 Poznań); e-mail: archiwum@poznan.ap.gov.pl; website: www.poznan.ap.gov.pl/

Schneidemühl (64-920 Piła) (branch of the Poznań archives); e-mail: pila@poznan.ap.gov.pl; website: www.poznan.ap.gov.pl/

Stettin (70-410 Szczecin); e-mail: sekretariat@szczecin.ap.gov.pl; website: www.szczecin.ap.gov.pl/

Thorn (87-100 Toruń); e-mail: archiwum@torun.ap.gov.pl; website: www.torun.ap.gov.pl/

You can check the availability of parish and civil records housed at the various Polish State Archives online at **http://baza.archiwa.gov.pl/sezam/pradziad.eng.php**.

(There are still over 150,000 Germans living in Poland.)

Russia and the Former USSR: Some church and civil records do exist for former areas of Germany or German settlements.

The State Committee on Archives in Ukraine has a good website called "Archives of Ukraine" at **www.archives.gov.ua/Eng,** which gives tips on accessing archives, genealogy research, and online resources. In addition, the Russian State Historic Archive (RGIA) in St. Petersburg contains many records of Germans who did business or worked in Tsarist Russia, were included in Russia because of boundary changes, or emigrated to Russia as colonists. The Archive was closed for two years while it relocated to a new building and is scheduled to reopen at the beginning of 2008 (check their website at **www.rusarchives.ru/federal/rgia** for the latest information). Their records can be accessed through the Russian Baltic Information Center (Blitz) at **http://feefhs.org/blitz/frgblitz.html**.

There are some records of genealogical interest in the National Archives in Washington, D.C., including the following:

> *Records of the Reichkommissar for the Baltic States 1941–45* (Microfilm T 459, rolls 3, 11, and 12).

> *Records of the Reich Ministry for the Occupied Eastern Territories 1941–45* (Microfilm T 454, rolls 1, 2, 3, 16, and 107).

These two series were microfilmed by the U.S. government at the end of World War II and contain details about archives in the Baltic states and Belarus. They include the records of the Civil Registry Offices (ZAGS) and a number of parish registers. There are no indexes to these records. The originals are in the Landeshautarchiv Koblenz, Karmeliterstrasse 1-3, 56068 Koblenz, Germany.

Two other websites that may be of some help are ArcheoBiblioBase's "Archives in Russia" at **www.iisg.nl/~abb**, which lets you search the archives of federal, regional, and local archives in Russia; and "Archives of Belarus" at **http://archives.gov.by/eng/**, which contains extensive information on the various archives in Belarus.

The state archives in the Baltic states of Estonia, Latvia, and Lithuania also contain Lutheran and Catholic church registers as well as civil registration records from 1919. The addresses of the archives are given below.

Estonia. The State Archives are located at Maneeži 4, 15019 Tallinn (e-mail: riigiarhiiv@ra.ee; website: www.riigi.arhiiv.ee/). The Estonian Historical Archives (J. Liivi 4, 50409 Tartu; e-mail: ajalooarhiiv@ra.ee; website: www.eha.ee) holds records of churches and educational institutions as well as manors and personal files. A database of Estonian family history archival sources is available online at **www.eha.ee/saaga**.

Latvia. There are three state archives in this country. The Latvia State Historical Archive (Slokas iela 16, 1048 Rīga; e-mail: histarch@latnet. lv; website: www.arhivi.lv/engl/en-dep-lvva.htm) holds records of the pre-Soviet period. The State Archives (Bezdelīgu iela 1, 1007 Rīga; e-mail: lva@lvarhivs.gov.lv; website: www.itl.rtu.lv/LVA) has records of the Soviet occupation period. The State Archive of Audiovisual Documents (Šmerla iela 5, 1006 Rīga; e-mail: arhivs@arhivs.apollo. lv; website: www.arhivi.lv/engl/en-dep-kino.htm) is also of interest to genealogists.

Lithuania. The state archives in Lithuania of interest to genealogists include the following two archives: the Central State Archives (Lietuvos centrinio valstybės archyvo, O.Milašiaus 21, LT 10102, Vilnius; e-mail: lcva@archyvai.lt; website: www.archyvai.lt/archyvai/index.jsp), which has birth, marriage, and death registers, wills, and land records; and the State Historical Archives (Lietuvos valstybės istorijos archyvas, Gerosios Vilties g. 10, LT 03134 Vilnius; e-mail istorijos.archyvas@lvia.lt; website: www.archyvai.lt/archyvai/index.jsp), which has vital records of the different religious communities up to the year 1940.

Germany only existed as an undivided country from 1871 until 1945—in contrast with England and France, which had been unified for more than five centuries. Systems of government in the various German states ranged from absolute monarchies to the near-democracy of some of the electorates and free cities. Various forms of confederation or economic grouping took hold, flowered for a few years, and died. Each state had its own laws, archives, and system of recording events. You cannot say, for example, that "censuses were first held in Germany in 1871." That is true for the unified Germany, but censuses were taken in Württemberg in 1821, in Baden in 1852, and so on. The only unified force in the Germanic area was the church—first the Catholic and later the Lutheran.

By the middle of the nineteenth century the number of self-governing German states had been reduced to thirty-four. Some of these formed the German Confederation, which also included Austria—still trying to assert its position as leader of the German people. However, the alliance was a shaky one because of the emerging power of Prussia, under the leadership of the great Bismarck. The two rivals did join together in an attack on Denmark in 1866 and seized Schleswig-Holstein, which they divided between them. A few months later they quarreled over the "spoils" and Prussia took over the whole territory. At this point Austria withdrew from the German Confederation and joined with Hungary in 1867 to form the Austro-Hungarian Empire.

The German Confederation was then renamed the North German Confederation under the leadership of Prussia, and included all the states north of the River Main. The eastern boundary was extended as far as Memel. In 1871, following a short and successful war against France, Prussia persuaded the southern states to join the Confederation with its new name of German Empire (Deutsches Reich). The king of Prussia was then proclaimed emperor on January 16, 1871. Suddenly, in the very center of Europe, a most powerful new country existed, and for the first time in over a thousand years the German people were one nation under strong leadership.

In the short period of a quarter of a century the German people had developed a pride in their nation, which was strong enough to overcome the hatreds and mistrusts of a thousand years of division and despair.

The new empire included the following territory:

(a) Kingdoms of Bavaria, Prussia, Saxony, and Württemberg;

(b) Grand Duchy of Baden;

(c) Free Cities of Bremen, Hamburg, and Lübeck, and Anhalt, Brunswick, Darmstadt, Hesse, Lippe, Mecklenburg, Oldenburg, Reuss, and the various states comprising Thuringia. (Justice, education, health, and police were left under the control of the individual states.)

During the period of unification between 1871 and 1945, little or no attempt was made to centralize records in one place such as the capital, Berlin. Instead, they remained in the capital cities of the original states. In retrospect, this was a blessing to ancestor-hunters because the destruction of German records during the Second World War was surprisingly small. Imagine what would have happened if everything had been in Berlin!

Details have already been given of the post-war dismemberment of Germany and the transfer of territory to Czechoslovakia, Poland, and the

USSR. The remaining part of Germany was then divided into the eastern half, occupied by the USSR, and the western half, occupied by Britain, Belgium, France, and the United States. These two parts later became the German Democratic Republic (Deutsche Demokratische Republik, or D.D.R.) and the Federal Republic of Germany (Bundesrepublik Deutschland, or B.R.D.). Details of the division were as follows:

D.D.R.: Anhalt, Brandenburg (western part), part of Brunswick (Braunschweig), Mecklenburg-Schwerin, Mecklenburg-Strelitz, Reuss, Sachsen-Altenburg, Sachsen-Meiningen, Sachsen-Weimar, Schwarzburg-Rudolstadt, and Schwarzburg-Sondershausen. Also four provinces of the State of Prussia (the parts remaining after territory taken by the three countries mentioned above).

B.R.D.: Baden, Bavaria (Bayern), part of Brunswick (Braunschweig), Coburg, Lippe, Oldenburg, Schaumberg-Lippe, part of Thuringia (Thüringen), Waldeck, Westphalia (Westfalen), and Württemberg; and five provinces of the State of Prussia—Hanover (Hannover), Hessen-Nassau, Rhineland (Rheinland), Schleswig-Holstein, and Sigmaringen.

After the division of Germany in 1945 various changes were made in each section of the country, and they were administered as follows:

D.D.R.: Originally this consisted of five provinces (Länder). These were abolished and replaced by fifteen districts (Kreise). However, the D.D.R., unlike the B.R.D., was not a federal state, and all power was centered in the capital (East, or Ost, Berlin).

B.R.D.: Originally this consisted of ten federal states (Bundesländer, or just Länder): Baden-Württemberg, Bavaria (Bayern), Bremen (city-state), Hamburg (city-state), Hesse (Hessen), Lower Saxony (Niedersachsen), North Rhine-Westphalia (Nordrhein-Westfalen), Rhineland-Palatinate (Rheinland-Pfalz), Saarland, and Schleswig-Holstein. The city-state of Berlin (West) was integrated into the legal and economic system of the Federal Republic. The republic was further divided into twenty-five administrative areas (Regierungsbezirke), 327 counties or districts (Kreise), and about 8,500 municipalities.

The sixteen states of the unified country and their capital cities are:
Baden-Württemberg (Stuttgart)
Bayern (Munich/München)
Berlin
Brandenburg (Potsdam)*
Bremen
Hamburg
Hessen (Wiesbaden)
Mecklenburg-Vorpommern (Schwerin)*
Niedersachsen (Hannover)

Nordrhein-Westfalen (Düsseldorf)
Rheinland-Pfalz (Mainz)
Saarland (Saarbrücken)
Sachsen (Dresden)*
Sachsen-Anhalt (Magdeburg)*
Schleswig-Holstein (Kiel)
Thüringen (Erfurt)*

The Länder marked with an asterisk (*) are the political divisions of the area previously known as East Germany. They replace the fifteen districts (Bezirkes) mentioned on the previous page. The names of the districts within each of the five Länder are:

BRANDENBURG: Berlin, Cottbus, Frankfurt, Potsdam
MECKLENBURG-VORPOMMERN: Neubrandenburg, Rostock, Schwerin
SACHSEN: Dresden, Chemnitz (formerly Karl-Marx-Stadt), Leipzig
SACHSEN-ANHALT: Halle, Magdeburg
THÜRINGEN: Erfurt, Gera, Suhl

THE CONTINUING MIGRATION

Earlier in this book I wrote about the great Germanic migrations in the Middle Ages and in the eighteenth and nineteenth centuries. After World War II approximately thirteen million Germans left their homes in other European countries and found refuge in the Fatherland. Since the unification of Germany and free emigration from the former Soviet Union and Eastern Europe, there has been a huge influx of ethnic Germans. Nearly 400,000 came in 1989, followed by more than 200,000 annually between 1991 and 1995.

The Germans in Kazakhstan may number as many as a million—some descended from the Germans who originally settled in the Volga Basin at the invitation of Catherine the Great, and others who were exiled from Ukraine by Stalin.

If you know you have German relatives in the former Soviet Union, Poland, or Romania you may be able to make contact through the International Red Cross or the Federal Ministry of the Interior in Bonn.

Starting the Family Tree

So—you have read the previous pages and your interest in your German ancestry has been aroused or rekindled. What *do* you do now?

You buy a genealogy software program or purchase a large sheet of white paper (about three by two feet) from a stationer or an art store, plus a three-ring binder. At the bottom of the sheet of paper you write your name and those of your brothers and sisters, if any, and any children. You also include dates and places of birth, marriage, and death. You write the names of your brothers and sisters in a horizontal line in descending order of age.

I am inventing an entirely imaginary Joseph Furst, whose family on both sides originated in "Germany," but he doesn't know when they emigrated or where they came from. He has often wondered about his German background but he has never got down to doing anything about it—mainly because he has no idea how to start, and also because he is afraid it may cost a lot of money.

When you have the names of your brother and sister written down, you add the dates of all the vital events (that is what we call births, marriages, and deaths) for them and their children and yours. The start of your family tree will look like the one on the following page for the imaginary Furst family:

JOSEPH
Born: 8 June 1920
Townsville WI
= Mary Johnson
(4 July 1947 Madison)

WILLIAM
Born: 13 January 1922
Townsville WI
= Catherine Spaak
(3 May 1944 Racine)

ANNA
Born: 2 February 1924
Townsville WI
= Herbert Whittaker
(23 March 1950 Avon)

JOHN
Born: 4
April 1949
= Bridget
May
(18 June
1975 Buf-
falo NY)

ERICA
Born: 3
Feb 1950
unmarried

MARIA
Born: 2 Jan 1945
= Mario Donizetti
(4 May 1965
New York NY)

RICHARD
Born: 11
Nov 1951
unmarried

HERBERT
Born: 11
Nov 1951
= Mary
Adams
(1 April
1974 Phila-
delphia PA)

PATRICK
Born: 11
Aug 1976
Madison

MAUREEN
Born: 4
Dec 1978
Madison

CESARE
Born: 3
Mar 1966
Ithaca NY

MARIA
Born: 2
Nov 1968
Ithaca NY

RICHARD
Born: 27
May 1976
Fargo ND

Next, you write in above all these entries the information you have about your mother and father:

JOHANN FURST
Born: 3 December 1895
Milwaukee WI

=

ERIKA BRAND
Born: 4 August 1896
Krefeld, Germany

(married on 5 May 1918 in the
Evangelical-Lutheran Church,
Milwaukee)

(*Note:* Always enter dates as they appear above—8/6/1920 can mean June 8 in one country and August 6 in another.)

Now your family tree is growing, and you turn your attention to your grandparents. At this stage you must decide whether you only want to trace the Furst family back or whether you prefer to trace the Brands, or both. There is no rule about this—you make the decision. If you decide to trace both the Fursts and the Brands, I suggest you deal with one family at a time. You will find it much easier to remember names and places as you go along. Of course, you will be writing everything down, but it is still better to concentrate on one side at a time. If you are looking down a long list of names one surname will spring out at you, whereas if you are looking for three or four you may easily miss one entry. An exception to this suggestion is if both your grandparents came from the same place—in that case, of course, you trace both families at the same time. However, you know your father was born in Milwaukee and your mother in Germany. It is easier to use the records here to start with, so father comes first.

Your sister reminds you that your father once said his father and mother spoke German to each other when they wanted to keep secrets, and that they both spoke English fluently but with an accent. This information does not help you very much—they may have been born in Germany or their German accents may have been because they spoke German at home as children, even though they were born here. You can never take anything for granted in ancestor-hunting—nor should you ever jump to a conclusion without checking for supporting evidence.

You have come up against your first obstacle. Was grandfather born in the United States or not? If he was German-born, where did he come from? Perhaps it wasn't in Germany at all. It is very likely he was born before 1871 (your father was born in 1895), and Germany did not exist as a separate country until that year.

How can you answer these questions? Your only living relatives here—apart from the next generation—are your brother and sister, and they have told you all they know, so what do you have? You know your own father was born in Milwaukee, and you have a copy of his birth certificate, which tells you his father's name was Josef Furst. Your father was born in 1895, and you remember he once told you he was only eight when his father died. So now you know you want to find out about a Josef Furst who was alive in 1895 and dead by 1903. You also know from the same certificate that his mother was Maria (née Ziegler). From the same source you know that Josef and Maria were living at 68 Heath Street, Milwaukee, when your father was born.

You search the Wisconsin Historical Society's online database of pre-1907 vital records, or you write to the Wisconsin Vital Records Office in Madison, Wisconsin and tell them you want a copy of the marriage certificate of Josef Furst and Maria Ziegler—believed to have been married in Milwaukee between 1890 and 1895. Of course, you don't know yet if the event did take place there or not, but your checking must start somewhere. They will send you a form to complete and will tell you the fee required, or you can download a form from their Internet site.

Your search of the marriage records for the period specified does not show an entry for the marriage. Now you know the odds are that the marriage took place in Germany. What is the next step? Census returns! These were taken on a statewide basis in Wisconsin from 1836, when it was a territory, to 1905 and are now in the custody of the Wisconsin Historical Society in Madison. You can request copies of the Wisconsin censuses from your local library's Interlibrary loan department, or you can write to the Wisconsin Historical Society, enclosing a self-addressed stamped envelope, and ask for details of the 1895 census return for 68 Heath Street, Milwaukee. For a small fee you will have opened up a whole new area of searching, and created new problems:

68 Heath Street Milwaukee

JOSEF FURST	age 38	Lutheran	Born Germany
MARIA FURST	age 37	Lutheran	Born Germany
JOHANN FURST	infant	Lutheran	Born Milwaukee

You can also check the available online databases to see if you can find information. For example, the Wisconsin Name Index, available on the Wisconsin Historical Society's website, searches obituaries, newspaper articles, and biographies between 1870 and 1970.

There are many other sources that can provide help—newspapers, passenger lists, land grants, etc. These will be found online and in various archives in Washington, D.C., and individual states and cities. Many are available on microfilm and can be borrowed through, and read in, your local library. In addition to these, you have church records and registers of the different denominations, which are in the individual churches or in the various church archives. These are usually located in the city where a bishop has his headquarters. There are also tombstones in churchyards and in public burial grounds which exist in most areas. Don't forget early newspapers (which often listed emigrants leaving the city or area), local histories (often only in manuscript form), and directories of inhabitants.

Last, but most certainly not least, is the vast collection of genealogical records acquired by The Church of Jesus Christ of Latter-day Saints (the LDS Church). You will find much more about these records later in this book. They do, in fact, include many of the official records I mentioned above.

One vital thing you must do is find out if someone—perhaps some unknown fifth or sixth cousin—has already traced your ancestors. You can try entering your surname into an Internet search engine, check the LDS website (**www.familysearch.org**), or contact the nearest LDS family history center and the public libraries and archives in the area from whence your ancestor came, and also in the area in which he or she settled. Make contact, too, with genealogical societies in the same areas. It would be a major tragedy if you were to spend a couple of years and, perhaps, a couple of hundred dollars tracing back your forebears, only to discover the search had already been made and you had never checked!

Let me give you an example of what may happen. Some years ago my wife and I decided to trace her grandmother's side of the family in Scotland—the name was Copland. We already had the information for four generations back, but beyond that all we knew was that the family had been living in the area of a city named Dumfries, in the southwest of Scotland. We were in the country at that time on a visit, and so we went to Dumfries prepared to spend a couple of weeks there visiting churchyards, churches, and so on. First of all, though, we went to the local library, met the librarian, and asked him, "Do you, by any chance, have information about a family named Copland that used to be prominent in this area a century and a half ago?" "Oh, yes," he replied. "I have a great deal of information about the family." He then produced a 400-page typed history of the family written by a family member fifty years earlier!

It was complete in every detail. The author had done his research most thoroughly and had meticulously recorded the source of all his information. Within thirty minutes we had found just where my wife's branch of the family fitted into the family history. From then on all the work had been done and there was a complete record of the family—documented and proved—back to a man named Ulf the Viking, Lord of Copeland, who had been alive in 1135. This took my wife's ancestry back twenty-four generations! If we had not checked with the library it would have taken us several years to go back that far. We also found that we were twenty-second cousins, or something like that, since I am descended from that same Viking through my Curwen ancestors.

Enough of the Baxters and the Coplands—let us go back to the Furst family. What are the basic facts you have to go on in your search in Germany? You know from the census return that both your grandparents were born in Germany in 1857 and 1858 respectively—*but* Germany did not exist until 1871. How can you find out exactly where they were born? Suddenly, you remember that often the place of birth was put on a tombstone. You know they died in Milwaukee and that your grandfather died about 1903. You get in touch with the office of the old public burial ground there and ask if they can possibly look at their records, see if your grandparents were buried there, and if so, if any place of birth appears on the tombstone. You realize, of course, that the odds are against you—they may have been buried elsewhere, there may be no information on the tombstone, it may not be possible to decipher the lettering, the staff of the burial ground may not be helpful.

You wait and wait for several weeks and then you get your answer.

> We have checked our records and find that on lot 39, avenue H46, is located the grave of Josef Furst and his wife, Maria. According to our records the information supplied by Mr. Furst's widow stated he had died on 12 May 1903, aged 46, and was interred on 16 May. Cause of death accidental. The grave also contains the remains of Mrs. Maria Furst (née Ziegler) who died 17 July 1916, and was interred on 21 July. Cause of death heart failure. Age 58. Information supplied by next of

kin (son) Johann Furst. A member of the staff has visited the grave site and it appears that Mr. Furst was born in Erlangen, Germany, in 1857, and Mrs. Furst in Nürnberg, Germany, in 1858.

Before you write to the church authorities in Germany you should check the LDS website (**www.familysearch.org**) or the nearest LDS family history center. The church has an ongoing project to copy all kinds of records of genealogical value in Germany. It may or may not have copied church records in the two places mentioned on the tombstone. If the registers have been microfilmed, you can borrow them through an LDS family history center and search them yourself there when the microfilms arrive from Salt Lake City. It is possible, too, that the church may have a computer printout of all Furst entries in the various Nürnberg church registers. The odds are against this being so, but check anyway.

If you are going to sit down and search the registers on microfilm yourself, you must be prepared for bad writing, faint writing, and, worst of all, the old Germanic script. There are several books available that explain script and German symbols used in the registers. I mentioned one of them at the beginning of this book, but there are others, and the library itself probably has at least one of them available.

If the LDS Church has not copied the church registers, you should now write to Germany—but where, you may ask, are Erlangen and Nürnberg? You can do a German town search online at "GOV—the genealogical gazetteer" (**http://gov.genealogy.net/**) or visit your nearest large library and look up a good indexed map of Germany. Either way, you will soon discover that Nürnberg is a large city in Bayern (Bavaria) and Erlangen a small town just outside. For the purpose of this particular example of a search, I have made the Fursts Evangelical-Lutherans, but they could just as easily have been Catholics—the procedure is the same.

Write to the Pastor (Herr Pfarrer), Evangelische-Lutherische Kirche, Erlangen. Cover the return postage, enclose a self-addressed airmail envelope, and offer to pay the fees required. Try and get your letter translated into German, and arrange for the reply to be translated as well. If you cannot do this then write in English. Be brief, be clear, be polite, and be grateful in advance:

Sehr geehrter Herr Pfarrer

I will be most grateful if you can check your register and let me know if you have a record of the baptism of Josef Furst between 1855 and 1860. If so, may I have a copy of the entry with all the details of parents, witnesses, addresses, etc., if they are given. I will pay whatever fee is required and thank you in advance for your kind assistance. A self-addressed envelope and three International Reply Coupons are enclosed.

Because Maria Ziegler came from Nürnberg, a big city with several churches, your letter will be worded differently and will go to the Sekretär, Landeskirchliches Archiv der Evangelisch-Lutherischen Kirche in Bayern (Veilhofstrasse 28, 90489 Nürnberg; e-mail: LKANuernberg@ t-online.de; website: www.lkan-elkb.de/)—these archives include material from most of the Evangelical-Lutheran churches in Nürnberg. In this case your letter will read:

> Sehr geehrter Herr Sekretär
> My grandmother, Maria Ziegler, was born in Nürnberg between 1857 and 1860. Unfortunately I do not know her address or the name of her parents, but I do know she was a member of the Evangelical-Lutheran Church. I think there are probably several churches in Nürnberg and will be most grateful if you can possibly ask the pastors of the churches to check their registers for her baptism. If the entry can be found I would like a copy with all the details of parents, witnesses, addresses, etc. if they are given. I will pay whatever fee is required and thank you in advance for your kind assistance. A self-addressed envelope and three International Reply Coupons are enclosed.

To save time, you can try e-mailing your request, using the e-mail contact form at **www.lkan-elkb.de/kontakt.php**.

Let us be optimistic and assume all goes well and you obtain all the information for which you asked. From this point you go steadily back via the marriage of the parents of Josef and Maria—through church registers and all the many other sources of information that are described in the following pages.

THE RECORDS OF THE LDS CHURCH

Anyone starting to trace his or her ancestors must make use of the vast genealogical collection of The Church of Jesus Christ of Latter-day Saints (the LDS Church). If you are tracing your German ancestors the LDS Church may be very valuable to you. It is not necessary to be a member of the church, or even to approve of its teachings, to be able to use its records.

Occasionally people have understandable fears about making contact with the church in their ancestor-hunt. They are afraid efforts will be made to convert them, and that an LDS elder may turn up on their doorstep one day to try to bring this about. This is not going to happen. The members of the church are extraordinarily nice, kind, helpful people, and your temporary association with them will do you no harm. I am not an LDS Church member, but over a great many years I have learned to appreciate their good qualities and the help I have received from many of them.

The interest of church members in genealogy stems from their theological belief that family relationships and family associations are intended to be eternal and not limited to a short period of mortal existence. Church members "sealed together" are not married only "until death do you part." It is believed that a husband and wife and their children remain together throughout eternity as a family unit with their ancestors and descendants.

Members of the church collect genealogical information about their ancestors in order to perform "sealing ceremonies" in temples erected for that purpose. Before the sealing of families from generation to generation can be performed, the families must be properly identified. This is done by members' own personal research and by using the records of the church—in particular the extraordinary collection of the Family History Library of The Church of Jesus Christ of Latter-day Saints (as it is officially known), located at 35 North West Temple, Salt Lake City, UT 84150 (for information call 801-240-2584; e-mail: fhl@familysearch. org; website: www.familysearch.org).

The library is engaged in the most comprehensive genealogical research program ever known. Microfilming and computerization are at the heart of the operation, and every day genealogical records are being copied, filmed, and preserved on microfilm and compact discs (CDs), and in computers. Documents such as parish registers, censuses, civil registration, land records, probate records and wills, marriage bonds, funeral sermons, military rosters, guild membership lists, school attendance records, cemetery records, and passenger lists are all being copied.

The statistics associated with the library are staggering in their immensity. The library contains over 2.4 million reels of microfilm; 742,000 microfiche; 310,000 books, serials, and other formats; 4,500 periodicals; and 700 electronic resources. These records contain nearly 2 billion names. If these figures amaze you, there is more to come! The collection grows by an average of 4,100 rolls of film, 700 books, and 16 electronic resources a month. Ancestral File™ records over 36 million names, while the International Genealogical Index™ (IGI) database contains approximately 600 million names, and an addendum to the IGI contains 125 million more names. The Pedigree Resource File™ database contains over 125 million names that are linked into families.

There are several ways that you can consult the vast collection of the LDS Church. You can visit the Family History Library in Salt Lake City or stop at one of the more than 4,000 branch family history centers operating throughout the world (check the LDS website at **www. familysearch.org/Eng/Library/FHC/frameset_fhc.asp**, or write to Salt Lake City at the above address, to find the location of the nearest family history center). If you want to look through the registers of the Evangelical Church of Hohenfriedeberg in Silesia (Schlesien), Grabau in Posen (Poznań), or Stallupönen in East Prussia (Ostpreussen); or get a list of everyone named Bernheim in the Evangelical Church registers of Dortmund between 1710 and 1915; or get information about Gerhard Eichler who was a goldsmith in Köln in 1785; or locate details of the next of kin who was a Feldwebel (sergeant) in the 18th Hussars in Vienna (Wien) in 1848—you can do all these things in your local family history center.

Increasingly, you can also do a considerable amount of research online at the LDS website: **www.familysearch.org**. This site allows you to search the following sources for family history information: Ancestral File; the International Genealogical Index; the Pedigree Resource File; the Family History Library Catalog; some census records; the U.S Social Security Death Index; Vital Records Index; a variety of guides to German research; and a guide to useful websites. In addition, you can browse a category list to find information about a specific family history topic or person; collaborate with others by sharing your family history information; submit GEDCOM files of ancestral information to the church for preservation; recommend a website to be included in the FamilySearch Internet Genealogy Service; purchase items produced by the church; and download the newest edition of Personal Ancestral File. The website is constantly updated, and new information is always being added.

The International Genealogical Index (IGI) is based on names copied from church registers in many different countries and is subdivided into countries or areas making up a country during a period of history. For the Germanic area this means separating the records so that each of the old kingdoms and principalities or dukedoms is separately indexed. The German section contains more than a quarter of a million names. It includes baptisms or births, marriages, and deaths or burials. However, you must bear some things in mind before using the IGI:

1. It only includes names taken from the records that have been copied—some church authorities will not cooperate with the LDS workers. In addition, the number of records to be copied is so great that in many areas only a percentage have, in fact, been copied. So always check whether the particular place in which you are interested is included in the IGI.

2. Copies are only as good as the person making the copy. Mistakes can be made, such as Wilhelm Müller being copied as Heinrich Müller. This is not so absurd as it sounds. One of my own ancestors appeared in the IGI for Lancashire, England as Thomas Caley, whereas the entry in the church register was Henry Caley. When I produced proof of the error, the LDS records were corrected. There can also be omissions caused by the worker turning over two pages of a register together and thus missing a whole page of entries.

I don't mention these incidents as criticism of the work of the LDS Church, but only to point out the possibility of human error. Don't accept the IGI as the final word. It can be invaluable but is not infallible! If you don't find the name of your ancestor where you are sure it should be, then check the original church register.

The IGI is available on microfiche, compact disc, and on the LDS website. The IGI is quite simple to use. The surname is on the left, followed in horizontal order across the page by the first name; the name of the wife or husband (if the entry is a marriage), or the names of the parents (if it is a baptism); the sex (M for a man, F for a woman); H for a husband, W for a wife; then the letter B for a birth or C for a christening, M for a marriage, N for a census, and W for a will. Finally, you arrive at the date of the event and the place.

Apart from the IGI, the most important LDS record is the Ancestral File. This contains what are called family group sheets. They are submitted by church members and are the result of their own research. They are further divided into two sections—main and patrons. The main sheets have been checked for accuracy, the patrons have not. All the sheets from both sections give the same type of information as in the IGI, plus dates of death and burial of parents, and the names of the grandparents. All these records are also available on microfilm through the various LDS family history centers, on compact disc, and on the LDS website.

Also available on compact disc is a lineage-linked database called the Pedigree Resource File. It contains family history records that individuals have submitted through the LDS website. The family information is organized in family groups and pedigrees and may include notes and sources. New names are constantly being added to this file. You can search the index to this database at **www.familysearch.org.**

Don't jump to conclusions about LDS records and say, "No member of our family has ever been a member of the LDS Church so there will be no point in checking the family group sheets." You may well have an unknown fourth or fifth cousin in the old country who is quite unknown to you. He or she may be a member of the LDS Church and may have traced the family back for many, many years.

In addition to the microfilms, the church has published many research papers containing genealogical information from many different countries. These can be downloaded free from the LDS website. Below are some of the booklets that contain information about Germany (check the LDS website for a complete list of titles):

Determining a Place of Origin in Germany
Genealogical Handbook of German Research
The German Empire Map, 1871 to 1918
German Genealogical Word List
German Letter-Writing Guide
Germany Research Outline
Hamburg Passenger Lists
Handwriting Guide: German Gothic
How to Use the Meyers Gazetteer
Latin Genealogical Word List
Modern Germany Map

If you are able to visit the library in Salt Lake City in person (more than 1,900 people do so every day), you will find more than 500 microfilm viewers available, and all the printed volumes are on open shelves. The parish registers are printed and indexed in alphabetical order.

The Family History Library does not do individual research, but it will answer specific questions. If you require detailed information, you will be mailed a list of researchers. When asking for this list be sure you specify your particular area of interest—you will then receive names and addresses of available researchers with knowledge of that area. At this point you make your own financial arrangements. However, bear in mind that you can do your own research on microfilm or microfiche in your nearest family history center, paying only a small fee for the purpose. So far as Germany is concerned, you may need a researcher's help as you get further back in time because of the style of writing and the German script used in earlier documents.

JEWISH RECORDS

In all my previous books I have included a separate section on Jewish records and this book is no exception. This policy does cause me misgivings—why not separate sections on Lutherans and Catholics and Mennonites? Why not separate chapters for Saxons and Bavarians and Swabians? Do my Jewish readers object to being singled out in this way?

However, "Jewish" is not just another religion, nor is it a distinct nationality—but the Jews are a separate people. They are separated by centuries of persecution, of subjugation, of pogroms, of the diaspora, of genocide, and finally, the concentration camps of World War II. They must be treated separately—their genealogical problems are not the same as those of other groups, their vital records are not always the same records. Their areas of research are more limited, or conversely are more widespread. Their vital events are not always recorded, or if they are, they may often be found in the records of other denominations because their own were not legally recognized.

What records will you find of Jews expelled from England in the Middle Ages—their synagogues sacked, their personal property stripped from them before they sailed? What records will there be of a child who survived a day when the Cossacks put his village to the torch and the sword? What records survive from the ghettos of a thousand Jewish settlements in Eastern Europe? What records can be found when, as recently as the middle of the last century, a Jewish family might have no family name?

Sometimes such records will exist in the most unlikely of places—be it in New York or Vienna or Tel Aviv. Yes, the problems facing Jewish ancestor-hunters are profound—but not insurmountable. There are three factors that must remain uppermost in your mind at all times: the records you need are not necessarily to be found in Jewish archives; every year new sources of information are being discovered; and you will have problems with family names.

In the German-speaking areas of Europe, the Jewish people were subject to the same civil laws of the various states as were any other citizens, both up to the unification of Germany and since then. Civil registration started for the whole new country in 1875, but it had existed for many years before that date in several of the individual states. In many areas west of the Rhine it started in 1810, in Hannover in 1809, in Prussia in 1870, to quote just a few examples. Remember, too, that in many areas Jews could record the vital events of the family—births, marriages, and deaths—within their own community, but this had no legal basis. To protect property rights and the validity of wills it was necessary they be recorded in the church of the state religion—be it Lutheran or Catholic. Sometimes a child's first name registered in a church differed from that recorded in a synagogue.

Probably the greatest problem facing the Jewish ancestor-hunter is that of family names, and you should give a great deal of thought and attention to this subject before you become too deeply involved in your search. Often, names were simplified or anglicized—Kanofsky became Kane, Moses became Morris, Martinez became Martin, and so on. Another complication is the literal translation of a name, so that Zevi in Hebrew became Hart in English and Hirsch in German.

Because the Jewish people, in the main, lived in isolated settlements throughout Europe from the Middle Ages onwards, there was not the pressing need for a family name. "Moses, son of Aaron" was a sufficient description for recognition in a small, tightly knit community. In some cases—particularly among the Sephardim—family names based on occupations did develop in the 1600s, but they were frequently only used within the family and had no legal validity. It was not until the latter part of the eighteenth century that family names as we know them were in general use among European Jews.

In 1787 Austria ordered that all Jews should have family names; Frankfurt-am-Main followed in 1808; Napoleon enforced a similar law in the areas under his control in 1808, while Switzerland did not pass any law on the subject until 1863. When the Jewish people had to decide on a family name, their decisions were based on a wide variety of facts or fancies. Inevitably, the most popular ones were based on occupations or personal descriptions or locations—so a tailor became a Snider, a tanner a Leder (leather), a carpenter a Nagel (nail), a small man was Klein, a short one Kurtz, a religious and God-loving man was Gottlieb, a man from the east was Osterman. There were many other variations—in Frankfurt, houses were distinguished by signs instead of numbers, so very many Jews took names based on the sign on their house, and a Jew living in a house with the sign of a red shield became Rothschild, or Schiff if his house had the sign of a ship. In certain areas, such as the northwestern part of Germany, the name Rose was very popular for some unknown reason, and so in these districts there was a preponderance of names like Rose, Rosen, Rosenkrantz, Rosenbloom, Rosengarten, and so on.

Further complications are the use of patronymics (names based on that of the father)—Lewis-sohn, Aaronson, Abrahamson, Myerson—and on matronymics (names based on that of the mother)—Perle, Perlson, Gutkind, and so on. Patronymics and matronymics were used, too, in a more general way—in Slavic areas Wicz or Vitch were added to the father's or mother's first name, in Romania it would be Vici, in German areas Sohn or Witz.

For the above reasons it is often difficult to trace your Jewish ancestry back beyond the 1700s unless you have some family documentation to guide you. You may even find that after your ancestors had a recognized family name they changed it to that of a revered rabbi or a well-known Talmudic scholar.

For a list of online databases and websites pertaining to German Jewish genealogy, go to **www.jewishgen.org/GerSIG/resources.htm#general**. Some useful addresses in Germany are:

Jüdische Presse
Postfach 04 03 69
10062 Berlin
Phone: 011-49-30-49988852
E-mail: buero@juedische-presse.de
Website: www.juedische-presse.de/

Jüdisches Dokumentationszentrum
Treibgasse 20
63739 Aschaffenburg
Phone: 011-49-60-2129087
E-mail: stadtarchiv@aschaffenburg.de
Website: www.aschaffenburg.de/

Jüdisches Kulturmuseum
Halderstrasse 8
86150 Augsburg
Phone: 011-49-8-21513658
E-mail: office@jkmas.de
Website: www.jkmas.de/

Jüdisches Museum Berlin
Lindenstrasse 9-14
10969 Berlin
Phone: 011-49-30-25993300

E-mail: info@jmberlin.de
Website: www.juedisches-museum-berlin.de/

Jüdisches Museum Westfalen
Julius-Ambrunn-Strasse 1
46282 Dorsten
Phone: 011-49-2-36245279
E-mail: info@jmw-dorsten.de
Website: www.jmw-dorsten.de/

Stiftung Neue Synagoge Berlin—Centrum Judaicum, Archiv (CJA)
Oranienburger Strasse 29
10117 Berlin
Phone: 011-49-30-88028425
E-mail: archiv@cjudaicum.de
Website: http://mysql.snafu.de/cjudaicum/index.html

Zentralarchiv zur Erforschung der Geschichte der Juden in Deutschland
Bienenstrasse 5
69117 Heidelberg
Phone: 011-49-6-221164141
E-mail: Zentralarchiv@urz.uni-heidelberg.de
Website: www.uni-heidelberg.de/institute/sonst/aj/index.html

So far as Jewish records in Europe are concerned, be sure you do not overlook the Hamburg Passenger Lists (see later in this book for full details), because this port and that of Bremen were the main places from which the emigrants from north and central Europe sailed to the New World. The Bremen records were destroyed by bombing in World War II, but the Hamburg lists exist from 1850 to 1934 (with the exception of Jan.–June 1853 and Aug. 1914–1919). The Bremen lists started in 1832 but lists from 1875-1908 older than three years were destroyed due to lack of space in the Bremen Archives. With the exception of 2,851 passenger lists for the years 1920-1939, all other lists were lost in World War II. The surviving lists have been transcribed in a joint project between the Bremen Chamber of Congress and a genealogical society called Die Maus, and they are now available online at **www.schiffslisten.de/index. php?lang=en.** In addition, a list of emigrants who sailed from Bremen to New York was compiled from U.S. sources by Gary J. Zimmerman and Marion Wolfert. Some 132,000 names for the period 1847–1871 have been collected and published (see Bibliography). You will also find online lists, transcribed from National Archives microfilms, of passengers from Bremen to New York and Bremen to Baltimore. For a list of these, go to **http://home.att.net/~wee-monster/onlinelists.html.**

If you already know the place from which your ancestors came, be sure you write to the local public library because many of the larger centers have Jewish collections containing a great deal of information about families in the area. These include detailed histories of Jewish communities. You will find that archivists and librarians are very helpful to Jewish inquirers from overseas. Try and overcome whatever deep-rooted feelings you may have and take advantage of these German sources—remember that most of the people you will be dealing with were born after the end of World War II.

The Weissensee Cemetery in Berlin is the largest Jewish cemetery in Europe. In the offices, there are over 115,000 index cards that give full details of each person buried there for over a century. You can obtain more details from Zentralarchiv zur Erforschung der Geschichte der Juden in Deutschland, Bienenstrasse 5, 69117 Heidelberg; e-mail: Zentralarchiv@urz.uni-heidelberg.de; website: **www.uni-heidelberg. de/institute/sonst/aj/index.html**.

The Hamburg Jewish Cemetery—dating back to 1611—is located on Konigstrasse and is being restored. There are 7,000 graves here; about one-third are those of Sephardic Jews. You can see some photos of the cemetery at **www.txmx.de/grafix/jufried**. A list of Jewish cemeteries in Germany is available online at **www.uni-heidelberg.de/institute/sonst/ aj/FRIEDHOF/belegexe.htm**. The Hamburg Staatsarchiv has a register of the Jewish community in that city dating back to 1769.

The International Tracing Service archive (ITS), located in Bad Arolsen, Germany (website: www.its-arolsen.org/english/index.html), has 30-50 million pages of documentation on 17.5 million victims of the Nazis (about a quarter of the records pertain to Holocaust victims). Until now, the archive has been closed to the public, but in August 2007 the first batch of digitized copies of the records were transferred to the United States Holocaust Memorial Museum in Washington, DC. The Museum will receive the records in three batches. The first batch contained documents from over 50 concentration camps and prisons, and included death books, transportation lists, and medical reports. Forced and slave labor records will be ready for transfer by early 2008, and displaced persons camp records should be completed in late 2008 or 2009.

Outside of Germany proper you will find Jewish records in other archives in what we call the Germanic area so far as language is concerned:

Austria

Jewish records are quite prolific for this country and are to be found in state archives, municipal offices, and magistrate's courts. For more information you should write to the Israelitische Kultusgemeinde

(Seitenstettengasse 4, 1010 Vienna; website: www.ikg-wien.at/). For example, there are the records of 300 synagogues in the Burgenland area in the provincial archives (Landesarchiv Burgenland, Freiheitsplatz 1, 7001 Eisenstadt). This area was part of Hungary until 1919 when it was ceded to Austria.

Hungary

There are a number of microfilms available of Jewish communities in the German-speaking areas of Hungary, and these are located in the National Archives of Hungary (Magyar Orzágos Levéltár, Bécsi kapu tér 4, 1014 Budapest; phone: 011-361-3565811; e-mail: info@mol.gov.hu; website: www.mol.gov.hu/). Yad Vashem (see below) has a computerized list of half a million Hungarian victims of the Holocaust.

Poland

Some of the various regional archives have Jewish records from what were German-speaking areas, such as Bytom (Beuthen), Kraków, Gdańsk (Danzig), Legnica (Liegnitz), Opole (Oppeln), Posnań (Posen), Warszawa (Warsaw), Wrocław (Breslau), Zielona Góra (Grünberg). Many of these have been microfilmed by the Central Archives in Jerusalem. Yad Vashem has a computerized list of 204,000 residents of the Lódź ghetto, with dates of birth, death, and deportation. (See below for addresses for the Central Archives and Yad Vashem.)

ISRAEL

There are a variety of sources in Israel:

Jewish National and University Library
Givat Ram Campus, Hebrew University
Jerusalem
Phone: 011- 972-2-6585027
Website: http://jnul.huji.ac.il/

Central Archives for the History of the Jewish People
Givat Ram Camus, Hebrew University
P.O. Box 39077
Jerusalem
Phone and Fax: 011-972-2-5635716
E-mail: archives@vms.huji.ac.il/
Website: http://sites.huji.ac.il/archives

The Douglas E. Goldman Jewish Genealogy Center/
The Nahum Goldmann Museum of the Jewish Diaspora
P.O. Box 39359, Tel Aviv 61392
Phone: 011-972-3-6405500. Fax: 011-972-3-6405727
E-mail: bhsemarc@post.tau.ac.il
Website: www.bh.org.il/Genealogy/index.aspx

Ghetto Fighters' House
D. N. Western Galilee, 25220
Phone: 011-972-4-9958080. Fax: 011-972-4-9958007
E-mail: simstein@gfh.org.il
Website: www.gfh.org.il/

Yad Vashem
P.O. Box 3477
Jerusalem 91034
Phone: 011-972-2-6443400. Fax: 011-972-2-6443443
E-mail: general.information@yadvashem.org.il
Website: www.yadvashem.org/

THE UNITED STATES

In the United States, you will find almost all of the records you need
for your German Jewish research. Outside New York City there are the
following organizations:

American Jewish Archives
3101 Clifton Avenue
Cincinnati, OH 45220
Phone: 513-221-1875. Fax: 513-221-7812
Website: www.americanjewisharchives.org/

American Jewish Historical Society
160 Herrick Road
Newton Centre, MA 02459
Phone: 617-559-8880. Fax: 617-559-8881
E-mail: info@ajhs.cjh.org
Website: www.ajhs.org/

The most dramatic development in Jewish record-keeping in North
America in recent years has been the creation of the Center for Jewish
History (15 West 16th Street, New York, NY 10011; phone: 212-294-
8301; fax: 212-294-8302; website: www.cjh.org). Five organizations
have joined together to establish what is destined to be the world center

for research into Jewish history—including, of course, Jewish genealogical research. Conceived in 1994 and opened in 2000, it cost $52 million. All but $4 million of this was raised by individuals, family trusts, and income from various events over the years of construction. The remaining money was a grant from the federal government.

The building encompasses 125,000 square feet of space in this five-section, multi-level complex. Online access is available to some of the holdings of the Center, which include documents, art, and artifacts, as well as a library. The computer system provides worldwide access to the treasures that are being accumulated from Israel, archival treasures of the member organizations, and individual collections.

The organizations housed in the Center for Jewish History facility are given below, with contact information:

American Jewish Historical Society; phone: 212-294-6160; fax: 212-294-6161; website: www.ajhs.org/

American Sephardi Federation; phone: 212-294-8350; fax: 212-294-8348; e-mail: info@americansephardifederation.org; website: www.americansephardifederation.org/

Leo Baeck Institute; phone: 212-744-6400; fax: 212-988-1305; e-mail: lbaeck@lbi.cjh.org; website: www.lbi.org/

Yeshiva University Museum; phone: 212-294-8330; fax: 212-294-8335; e-mail: info@yum.cjh.org; website: www.yumuseum.org/

YIVO Institute for Jewish Research; phone: 212-246-6080; fax: 212-292-1892; website: www.yivo.org/

(The Leo Baeck Institute specializes in the German-speaking areas of Europe; the YIVO Institute specializes in East European Jewry.)

The New York Public Library (Dorot Jewish Division)
Fifth Avenue at 42nd Street, New York, NY 10018
Phone: 212-930-0601; fax: 212-642-0141
Website: www.nypl.org/research/chss/jws/jewish.htm

This has one of the largest collection of Judaica in the world, and the second largest collection of yizkor books in the city (second only to the YIVO Institute). It is impossible to list all the holdings, but the German collections include tombstone inscriptions from Köln, Nürnberg, Speyer, and Worms; genealogies from Germany and Lithuania; and records of many Jewish communities from the Germanic areas of Europe. You could happily and profitably spend two or three days here. The majority of their yizkor books are available online at **www.nypl.org/research/chss/jws/yizkorbooks_intro.cfm**.

There are two other organizations in the city that may also be of value to you: The Jewish Theological Seminary Library (3080 Broadway, New York, NY 10027; website: www.jtsa.edu/Library.xml) and the Mendel Gottesman Library of Hebraica and Judaica (Yeshiva University, 2520 Amsterdam Avenue, New York, NY 10033; website: www.yu.edu/libraries).

The National Archives at College Park (8601 Adelphi Road, College Park, MD 20740; phone: 301-837-2015; fax: 301-837-0483; website: www.archives.gov/dc-metro/college-park/) holds over 70,000 rolls of microfilm of captured German records and related documents, including registers of German concentration camp inmates and index cards filmed at the Berlin Document Center listing the name, date and place of birth, occupation, and last address of Jews whose German citizenship was revoked in accordance with the Nürnberg Laws of 1935.

CANADA

The Canadian Jewish Congress Charities Committee (CJCCC) National Archives
1590 Docteur Penfield Avenue
Montreal, Quebec, H3G 1C5
Phone: 514-931-7531. Fax: 514-931-0548
E-mail: archives@cjccc.ca
Website: www.cjccc.ca/national_archives
The CJCCC archives collects and preserves documentation on all aspects of the Jewish presence in Quebec and Canada.

Jewish Genealogical Society of Canada
P.O. Box 91006
2901 Bayview Avenue
Toronto ON M2K 2Y6
E-mail: info@jgstoronto.ca
Website: www.jgstoronto.ca/

For a list of repositories and resources pertaining to Holocaust research in Canada, go to **www.jgstoronto.ca/Holocaust.html**.

Finally, do not be discouraged by your Jewish ancestral difficulties—bring to the search the tenacity, the patience, the determination, the intelligence, and the deep attachment to history of your ancestors.

ARCHIVES

Later in this book we will be talking about archives—those often mysterious places that hold many of the secrets of our ancestry. You will read about national archives, provincial archives, state archives, district archives, county archives, city archives, church archives, industrial archives, and even family archives. If you visit archives in person you will find they vary greatly—some are beautiful modern buildings, all glass and light, equipped with computers and microfilm readers, with charming, helpful archivists going out of their way to be helpful. Others look like something left over from the Middle Ages, with dusty shelves and even dustier books hidden away in dark corners and illuminated with 40-watt bulbs—presided over by unfriendly archivists who regard their treasures as their own personal property and you as an unwelcome visitor to be gotten rid of as quickly as possible.

It is impossible within the limited space of this book to list all the holdings of each individual archive, although I have done my best to cover all the main sources of information you will find. However, two of the many German archives must be discussed in some detail because (a) they are not widely known and may be overlooked, and (b) they have material of great value to people whose forebears came from some of the "lost territories" of Germany—Prussia (Ost und West Preussen), Silesia (Schlesien), Posen (Poznań), Pomerania (Pommern), the Sudetenland, Estonia (Estland), and Latvia (Lettland). The latter two countries also include areas that no longer exist as separate entities—Courland (Kurland) and Livländ (Livonia).

These two archives I mention are the Herder-Institut in Marburg (Lahn) and the Evangelical Church Archives in Berlin.

Herder-Institut
Gisonenweg 5-7, 35037 Marburg
Phone: 011-49-6-421184140. Fax: 011-49-6-421184139
E-mail: herder@herder-institut.de
Website: www.herder-institut.de/

The Herder-Institut, founded in 1950, is one of German's principal centers for historical research on East-Central Europe. As I mentioned earlier, German settlements were established in the Baltic area as early as the time of the Crusades. Over the years the German areas in Estonia and Latvia were almost independent of the host countries. They maintained their language, their social customs, and their religion (mainly Protestant). In 1939 a treaty was signed between the German government and the two Baltic states, in which it was agreed that the records of the German settlements and churches could be filmed. Soon after the work began, the USSR took over the two countries, plus Lithuania, and incorporated them into the Soviet Union. However, the copying of the records continued until 1941. Lithuania was not included in the arrangements as the German areas in that country were practically nonexistent except for Memel.

In Estonia (Estland), a very large part of the material in the State Archives in Tallinn (Reval) and Tartu or Yurev (Dorpat) was copied. This material contains much information about the early German settlements in those areas, and includes records of the University of Dorpat; the city archives of Reval, including lists of citizens and property records; and records of the various craft guilds. The material was transferred to Berlin in 1941 and 1942, and a little later more than 700 rolls were sent to Posen (now Poznań, in Poland) where it was intended that a center for German-Baltic culture would be built after the war. In 1944 the records were transferred to Brunswick (Braunschweig) and came into the custody of the British army a year later. They were kept at Goslar until 1950 and were then transferred to the custody of the Baltic Historical Circle in Göttingen, and finally to the Herder-Institut in 1952.

In Latvia (Lettland), nearly all the German records in the State Archives in Riga were filmed as well as those in the city archives. The latter included the registers of members of the various guilds, rolls of citizens from 1614 to 1812, rent books, land records and deeds, and a variety of other municipal records. From the areas of Latvia known as Courland and Livonia a number of "Seelenlisten" (church membership rolls) were also filmed, covering a period from the late eighteenth century until the middle of the nineteenth.

The films from Latvia reached the Herder-Institut in the same roundabout way as those from Estonia.

Other miscellaneous records in the Institut include some family papers and family trees from Pomerania (Pommern), extracts from some church books (Kirchenbücher) from the same area—in particular from Schlawe from 1618 to 1710—and a few of these books from Silesia (Schlesien). There are also the family and business papers of Gerhard Lange, from Schlawe, in which he mentions many individuals and families in that area during the last century. Finally, there is a small collection of biographies from the Sudetenland (now in the Czech Republic).

The films and manuscripts here, together with other items in the State Archives in Koblenz, form a unique collection of material for German-Baltic research. Some of the records in both locations have been filmed by the LDS Church. It consists mainly of Seelenlisten from Courland (Kurland) and Livonia (Livländ). The Acquisitions Division of the LDS library will be able to supply you with up-to-date information about this potentially valuable and continuing project.

I am sorry I do not have space to list the holdings of the Institute in greater details because it is a treasure-trove of information about the centuries of German occupation of Estonia and Latvia (Livonia and Curland). However, I do suggest you visit their website to check out their online databases and listing of holdings, and to download at no cost a book published by the Institut that does go into very great detail: *Archivbestande zur Geschichte Liv-, Est -und Kurlands in der Dokumentesammlung-des Herder-Instituts.* However, it is in German, which may be difficult for you.

Evangelisches Zentralarchiv in Berlin (EZA)
Bethaniendamm 29, 10997 Berlin
Phone: 011-49-30-22504520. Fax: 011-49-30-22504540
Website: www.ezab.de/

One of the great adventure stories of genealogy is that of the successful removal of the great majority of the church registers (Kirchenbücher) of the Evangelical Church from the "lost territories" of Prussia, Posen, Pomerania, and Silesia in 1944 and their eventual safe haven in the central archives of the church in Berlin. These priceless treasures are not only of great value to ancestor-hunters, but also to Germans seeking to prove the dates of vital events in order to claim pensions and to obtain passports and inheritances. Almost all of the Kirchenbücher have been microfilmed by the LDS Church (which also played a large part in the preservation of the original registers).

The collection now in Berlin consists of about 7,000 parish registers from more than 500 different parishes in the territories mentioned above; 763 records from the Military Church Registers of the former Prussian army and the German Wehrmacht; and 70 parish registers from German-speaking congregations outside of Germany. There is no comprehensive index, but a number of the individual books were indexed by the ministers of the particular parishes. Sometimes this covers an extended period of several centuries, but often it only includes more recent entries. In addition, the EZA publishes catalogs that list the church books in their collection (see www.ezab.de/e/eaframe.html for details). You can obtain detailed information about a parish from your nearest LDS family history center, or directly from Salt Lake City. The authorities at the Berlin archives will not undertake searches for individual names but will answer a simple inquiry. You can visit the reading room and consult the parish registers in person if you make a seat reservation two to three months in advance. Reservations can be made in writing by postal mail, fax, or e-mail (Kirchliches Archivzentrum in Berlin, Bethaniendamm 29, 10997 Berlin; fax: 011-49-30-22504540; e-mail: reservierung@ezab.de).

In the fall of 1944, when it became obvious that the area was in danger of invasion, the church authorities in the various centers—Königsberg (now Kaliningrad), Danzig (Gdańsk), and Stettin (Szczecin)—ordered the ministers of the Evangelical churches to bring all records for shipment to the west in the area of Rhon (near Frankfurt). The great majority of the ministers complied and the books were stored in mine shafts. After the war the Kirchenbücher were damaged by thieves and arsonists, and many were destroyed. No list had been made of the books deposited, so it is not known which were stolen or destroyed and which were retained in the original churches. It is very fortunate that the books from the main centers such as Königsberg (with nineteen parishes) and Stettin (with twenty-two) are virtually complete. There are some records from Danzig but they are by no means complete. A number of the books there were handed over to the church authorities in 1943, but many ministers refused to surrender them when requested. There was a local dispute at the time because some believed the records would be used to discover which inhabitants were Aryan and which were non-Aryan.

At the end of World War II, Paul Langheinrich, a member of the LDS Church, instituted a search for church books and records in the areas occupied by the Soviet forces. He was very successful in this effort and later obtained permission from the Soviet government to take all the books he had found to Berlin. The Red Army even provided a truck for this purpose.

At the same time, the LDS Church entered into negotiations with the Evangelical Church. The LDS officials explained they had no wish to retain the books when they discovered them, but only to copy them before returning them to the church. The Evangelical Church agreed to this and fully cooperated with the researchers of the LDS Church. At this time more Kirchenbücher were recovered from the areas I have mentioned and also from areas outside Prussia and Pomerania such as Posen and Silesia.

The Kirchenbücher available for Prussia and Pomerania are too numerous to list in this book, but there is space available to give details of the books from Silesia and Posen. Please bear in mind that the fact that a parish is mentioned does not mean that the records are complete, or that they cover a long period of time, so don't be too excited if you find the name of your ancestral town or village mentioned.

SILESIA (SCHLESIEN): Bunzlau, Goldberg, Grüssau, Hohenfrideberg, Karzem, Königszelt, Leopoldshain, Liegnitz, Marklissa, Reinersdorf, Rothenburg.

POSEN (POZNAŃ): Bromberg, Brostrowe-Friedheim, Cielle, Debenke, Fordon, Gogolin, Grabau, Gross Neudorf, Grünkirch, Krone-an-der-Brahe, Lobsens, Mrotschen, Nakel, Otterau-Langenau, Raschkow, Runowo, Sadke, Schulitz, Schweinert, Schwerin-an-der-Warthe, Sienno, Stenschewo, Weichselhorst, Weissenhöhe, Wilhelmsort, Wirsitz, Wissek, Zduny, Zinsdorf, Zirke.

Some Prussian records were transferred from Merseburg (Sachsen-Anhalt) to Berlin. They include property deeds. Although the records bear the title Secret State Archives Prussian Cultural Heritage Foundation (Archivstrasse 12-14 14195 Berlin; phone: 011-49-30-83901-00; e-mail: gsta.pk@gsta.spk-berlin.de; website: www.gsta.spk-berlin.de/), they are open for genealogical research.

Berlin Document Center
Department of German Reich
Finckensteinallee 63
12205 Berlin
Phone: 011-49-1888-770-411. Fax: 011-49-1888-7770-111
E-mail: berlin@barch.bund.de
Website: www.bundesarchiv.de/aufgaben_organisation/abteilungen/reich/00340/index.html

The Berlin Document Center contains the most comprehensive collection of Nazi files for 1933–45. The collection of 30 million documents includes the membership files of some 10 million members of the Nazi Party, as well as personnel files of 600,000 Storm Troopers, 350,000 members of the S.S., and 60,000 S.S. officers. Control of this archive was transferred from the United States to Germany in 1994.

Under the terms of the United States–Germany agreement all documents were microfilmed before the transfer and are available for public search at the National Archives at College Park (8601 Adelphi Road, College Park, MD 20740; phone: 301-837-2015; fax: 301-83-0483; website: www.archives.gov/dc-metro/college-park/).

THE LUTHERAN CHURCH

Since your German ancestors may have been members of the church in both the Germanic area of Europe and later in North America, you should be aware of changes that took place in 1986 in the organization of the church in both the United States and Canada. The various mergers that took place may change the locations of the church headquarters in both countries. This may also have an effect on the location of the church archives.

In the United States three Lutheran churches agreed to merge into a single church—the Evangelical Lutheran Church in America (ELCA), with national headquarters in Chicago. The three churches concerned were the Lutheran Church in America, the American Lutheran Church, and the Association of Evangelical Lutheran Churches. The Lutheran Church-Missouri Synod remains outside the new church because it is more conservative and does not practice open communion or allow women to be ordained as ministers. They are also more literal and conservative in their interpretation of the scriptures.

In Canada the three districts of the Lutheran Church in America acted jointly through the Lutheran Church in America—Canada Section. The Canadian counterpart of the American Lutheran Church has been independent since 1971 and was known as the Evangelical Lutheran Church of Canada (ELCC). The ELCC and the three synods of the Lutheran Church in America merged on January 1, 1986 and are now called the Evangelical Lutheran Church in Canada (ELCIC). The church headquarters are located at 302-393 Portage Avenue, Winnipeg, MB R3B 3H6 (website: www.elcic.ca). There are a few other Lutheran groups in Canada, which total about one percent of the Lutheran population.

The Lutheran Church—Canada was founded in 1988 when the Canadian congregations of The Lutheran Church—Missouri Synod formed an autonomous Canadian church with three districts, one in Edmonton, Alberta; one in Regina, Saskatchewan; and one in East District in Kitchener, Ontario.

THE GERMANS IN THE UNITED STATES

Although the major period of German immigration into North America was in the nineteenth century, the first mass entry of German colonists was in 1683 when Germantown, in Pennsylvania, was founded. Even so, the description "mass" is a misnomer, since the party totaled thirteen families. However, it is easier to use the word "mass" to describe organized bodies of immigrants as opposed to the scattered entry of individuals or small family groups. It is quite possible that individual Germans landed before 1683, but we have no certain record of their arrival, although rumor has it that the earliest German settlers were in Virginia and Maryland as early as 1608.

From the early eighteenth century to the nineteenth century Germans settled in many states besides the three I have mentioned above—notably New York, the Carolinas, Texas, Wisconsin, Ohio, and Illinois. In this brief account of German immigration we must confine ourselves to major areas of settlement rather than attempting a complete history of all fifty states, or even those in the original thirteen colonies.

German settlement really commenced with the arrival of the "Palatines" in 1709 and their settlement in the colony of New York. Although the description "Palatine" really applied only to people from the Palatinate area of the Rhineland (now known as the state or land of Rheinland-Pfalz), it was also used to describe people from Baden, Bavaria (Bayern), Alsace (Elsass), Hesse (Hessen), and Württemberg.

There were a number of reasons for the great migrations—poor crops, bad winters, heavy taxes, military service, religious persecution, and most of all, the devastation caused by the Thirty Years War (1618–1648) and subsequent invasions of the Rhineland by France in 1673, 1688, and 1707. The winter of 1708–09 was the worst in Europe in more than a century. The intense cold started in October and continued until the end of April, and the vines and fruit trees in the southwest of the German area were destroyed. According to contemporary accounts, birds died in the air and spittle leaving the mouth was ice before it reached the ground. The disaster was total and the future without hope.

The Palatines started to arrive in London, England, via Rotterdam in 1708, and in 1709, according to some reports, 30,000 arrived between May and October. The refugees arriving in England had every intention of continuing their journey as soon as possible to Pennsylvania and the Carolinas. Representatives of these colonies had been active in the Rhineland proclaiming the attractions of good land and low taxes. William Penn himself paid several visits to the area, and in 1681 leaflets were distributed offering land in Pennsylvania at the price of two English pounds for 100 acres.

However, the English government, faced with a multitude of refugees beyond all expectations, blew hot and cold on the project. Objections were raised by English settlers already in the colonies and efforts were made to arrange settlement on various islands in the Caribbean, in England itself, and in Ireland. Meanwhile the Palatines continued to pour into London, and tented camps were set up in the suburbs, and houses, barns, and warehouses were requisitioned or donated.

Eventually some 3,000 Protestants were persuaded to settle in Ireland, where the policy of the English government was to dispossess the Catholic peasants and replace them with Protestants. By January 1710 more than 2,000 of the original 3,000 had settled in Co. Limerick and Co. Dublin, but another thousand had returned to London. Those remaining were given eight acres of land for every member of the family.

The great John Wesley, founder of the religious movement that bears his name, visited a Palatine community in Co. Limerick in 1760. He records in his journal: "I rode over to Killiheen, a German settlement, nearly twenty miles south of Limerick. In the evening I preached to another colony of Germans at Ballygarane. The third is at Court Mattrass, a mile from Killiheen. There is no cursing or swearing, no Sabbath-breaking, no drunkenness, no ale-house in any of them. How will these poor foreigners rise up in the judgement against those that are round about them." In spite of their difficulties, they survived, and there are many descendants in the area today with names like Switzer, Heck, Miller, and Shire.

Meanwhile, those left in London were living under very poor conditions—financial aid from the English government was minimal, but it was augmented by private donations obtained by the efforts of the Church of England. Inevitably, the refugees were accused of becoming a financial burden, of taking jobs away from the English, and even of introducing the plague into the country. Several of the camps and settlements were attacked by the London mobs and a number of Palatines were killed or wounded.

The leader of the first contingent to arrive in 1708 was the Rev. Joshua Kocherthal. His party consisted of forty-one people from Landau, in the Palatinate, and fourteen more from the same place joined them a few weeks later. It was eventually decided they should settle on the Hudson River, in the New York colony, some fifty miles north of New York City. They sailed in mid-October 1708 and took nine weeks on the voyage. Their settlement was named Newburgh.

By mid-summer of 1709 the Palatines were arriving at Rotterdam at the rate of a thousand a week. From there they were shipped to England in transport ships that had brought soldiers over to the Netherlands to fight in the War of the Spanish Succession. In September the English became worried about the number of Catholics among the refugees and some 3,000 were sent back to the Rhineland with a parting gift of five Dutch guilders.

In January 1710 the first mass sailing to the New World took place— some 600 Palatines left for the Carolinas and later founded the settlement of New Bern. In April 3,000 more sailed for New York. Eighteen hundred of them settled on the Hudson some ninety miles north of the city, while the balance stayed in the city itself. In 1712 the financial subsidies from the colonial government to the Hudson River settlers were abruptly ended. They were told they could hire themselves out as servants in New York or New Jersey but nowhere else. During the next five years many of them crossed into Pennsylvania, while others settled in Albany, Schenectady, and in Schoharie, on the Mohawk.

From 1717 onwards there was a steady stream of settlers into Pennsylvania, both from New York and directly from England. Many settlements were established in the eastern part of the colony between the Susquehanna and Delaware rivers and around the fast-growing city of Philadelphia. Pennsylvania was "the promised land" for the Germans—both those waiting in England and those now sailing directly from European ports. There were liberal terms for land purchase, religious toleration, and the existence of established German settlements and a way of life that made the colony irresistible.

Between 1727 and 1775 nearly 70,000 Germans went to Pennsylvania. A little earlier—in 1710—they had begun to enter Maryland in large numbers, and by 1756 the majority of the population was estimated to be of German origin. The main cause of this sudden departure from Pennsylvania was Indian attacks on the isolated German settlements and the refusal of the Quaker government to provide firearms for their protection. The main area of settlement was around Frederick and along the Monocacy River. At about the same time (1709–1729) small settlements were also established in Virginia and North Carolina. It is estimated that 200,000 Germans immigrated to North America in the eighteenth century and more than three million in the nineteenth. At the time of the Revolution nearly ten percent of the population was of German origin. In Pennsylvania German came close to being declared the official language.

Immigration tapered off towards the end of the eighteenth century because of industrialization in the German areas of Europe and consequent increased prosperity. There were also official restrictions on emigration in many of the states that were later to form the unified country of Germany, and an increase in compulsory military service. However, the pause was short-lived. By 1818 one bad harvest had followed another, the Napoleonic Wars had taken their toll of life and property, and religious disputes within the Lutheran Church had led to ill feeling and a disruption of orderly life. All these events led to another wave of emigration—this time from Bavaria (Bayern) and Württemberg, and later from Hesse (Hessen), Thuringia (Thüringen), and West Prussia (Westpreussen). By 1840 all the Germanic areas were contributing to the floodtide, but the majority still came from the southwest—mainly because of the history of close association with America and family connections with those already established in the great republic beyond the ocean.

The religious disputes I mentioned above were caused in the main by a compulsory union of the Reformed and Lutheran churches ordered by King Frederick William III of Prussia. A breakaway sect opposed to union and known as the "Old Lutherans" took the lead in the new emigration. More than a thousand went to the United States in 1839—700 to Wisconsin and the rest to Buffalo. In 1847 a large organized party left Lippe-Detmold in the North Rhineland for Missouri and Wisconsin, and in the following year more Missouri settlements were established by immigrants from Westphalia (Westfalen) and Hamburg. Smaller family groups went to the cities of Milwaukee and Cleveland.

At this time many Germans who were destitute had their passage overseas paid by their local community to save the increasing costs to the public purse. In the early 1840s a number of emigrant societies (generally known as Auswanderungsverein) were set up in various parts of the German area. They were organized on a cooperative self-help basis with the support of the various state governments. Their objectives were to help members to emigrate, and this help included both money and advice. The records of many of these societies—but by no means all—are in the state or city archives in Germany, together with copies of early newspapers devoted to the subject of emigration. The main centers were in the following places (the name of the existing state is given in parentheses):

Berlin
Breslau (now Wrocław, in Poland)
Darmstadt (Hessen)
Düsseldorf (Nordrhein-Westfalen)
Frankfurt-am-Main (Hessen)
Giessen (Hessen)
Hannover (Niedersachsen)
Karlsruhe (Baden-Württemberg)
Leipzig (Sachsen)
Mainz (Rheinland-Pfalz)
Stuttgart (Baden-Württemberg)

The high points in immigration into the United States in the nineteenth century were in 1854 when more than a quarter of a million Germans arrived, and in the period 1866–1873. The latter years saw the emergence of Prussia (Preussen) as the dominant state in the German area and a series of wars against Austria, Denmark, and France, culminating in the proclamation of the German Empire in 1870. In 1880 more than 200,000 Germans immigrated to North America. The estimates—and they can be no more than that—are that between 1820 and 1900 the number of immigrants totaled between three and five million.

Since those days there has been a steady flow of German immigrants, but not on the same scale. The end of constant wars between the various states, the unification of Germany, and the end of cheap land in the United States all made the Fatherland a more attractive place in which to live, and this was reflected in smaller immigration figures. In 1900 the annual total was down to 20,000.

The main ports used by immigrants from Europe were New York, Philadelphia, Boston, Baltimore, and New Orleans. Some passenger lists for these ports do exist and you will find details later in this book. More information can be obtained from the National Archives in Washington and its regional archives.

The ports used in Europe by emigrants consisted of several major ones and a number of small harbors such as Danzig (Gdańsk), Lübeck, Rostock, and Stettin. Practically no records exist of passengers leaving the smaller ports, but lists are available in various places for some of the main ports, and in most cases copies have been made by the LDS Church. These ports are listed below with the location of the archives containing the records where they still exist:

Hamburg (1850–1934, except 1 Jan.–14 July 1853 and the WWI years of 1915–1919), Staatsarchiv Hamburg, Katlunbleiche 19, 22041 Hamburg, Germany. Online images for the Hamburg passenger departure records from 1850-1934, as well as a partial index to the records, can be viewed for a subscription fee at Ancestry.com (http://content.ancestry.com/iexec/?htx=List&dbid=1068). See the "Records in Germany" chapter for more information about these passenger lists.

Göteborg (1876–1913), Landsarkivet, P.O. Box 19035, Geijersgatan 1, 400 12 Göteborg, Sweden; website: www.statensarkiv.se/

Antwerp (1854 and 1855), Rijksarchief, Door Verstraeteplein 5, 2018 Antwerp, Belgium; website: http://arch.arch.be/

Le Havre (1749–1830), Archives départmentales de la Seine-Maritime, Cours Clemenceau, 76101 Rouen Cedex, France; website: http://www.archivesdepartementales76.net/

Bordeaux (1713–1787), Archives départementales de la Gironde, 13-25 rue d'Aviau, 33081 Bordeaux Cedex, France; website: http://archives.cg33.fr/

Bremen records started in 1832 but lists from 1875-1908 older than three years were destroyed due to lack of space in the Bremen Archives. As noted earlier, all but 2,851 passenger lists for the years 1920-1939 were destroyed by British bombing in World War II. The surviving lists have been transcribed in a joint project between the Bremen Chamber of Congress and a genealogical society called Die Maus, and are now available online at **www.schiffslisten.de/index.php?lang=en.** There are also a few copies of Bremen passenger lists in the State Archives in Koblenz (Karmeliterstrasse 1-3, 56068 Koblenz).

It must be pointed out that the passenger lists in the various ports mentioned above have not all been indexed, and in order to obtain details it may be necessary to provide the name of the ship and the date of sailing. In some cases, indexing is now being done and you should check with the authority concerned for more detailed and up-to-date information.

When researching your ancestors in passenger lists you must always be on the lookout for name changes—misspellings, names written as they sounded, names simplified, names changed accidentally or deliberately by immigration officers, names that were anglicized, etc. Here are just a few examples taken at random:

Bekker	Baker	Roth	Ross
Brunn	Brown	Schmitt or	
Heinrich	Henry	Schmidt	Smith
Hellmann	Hill	Schneeburger	Snow
Jong	Young	Stein	Stone
Konig	King	Wasser	Waters
Loewen	Lowe	Werfer	Weaver
Mann	Manning	Werner	Warner
Rickert	Richards		

Finally, while we are on the subject of names, remember diminutives (first names that are shortened) or "pet" names that bear little resemblance to the original. Here are a few examples:

Georg	Yuri, Jorg	Philip	Lipsi
Heinrich	Henni	Renate	Reni
Johann	Hansi	Rosina	Sina
Josef	Seppi	Rudolf	Dolf or Folph
Matthias	Tice	Wilhelm	Villie

As you are of German descent you should always remember that your ancestor may have settled in the United States after a brief stay in Canada, or he may have emigrated from the United States to Canada. Among many early Mennonite settlers there was a great deal of movement backwards and forwards across an unsupervised and unregulated border, and also many arranged marriages between a man settled in Ontario, Canada, and a woman in Pennsylvania or New York—or vice versa.

If you are not of Mennonite descent, then you may still come into cross-border problems because of the close friendship of Lutheran families in the two countries. An additional problem may possibly stem from a descent from one of the "Hessians"—the soldiers from the German area of Europe who fought in the British army during the American Revolution. The term "Hessian" is a misnomer. In fact, the German mercenaries came from many places in the Germanic area besides Hesse. They came from Brunswick, Anhalt-Zerbst, Anspach-Bayreuth, Prussia, Württemberg, and in fact from many other areas of Europe, including Austria, Estonia, Latvia, Hungary, and Italy.

After the United States became independent the German soldiers went their separate ways—some went back to their homes in Europe, some stayed in the United States, and many others crossed the border into Canada. Because of this general dispersal it has always been difficult to arrive at an estimate of their numbers, but it seems likely that at least 10,000 settled in Canada, where they were treated in the same way as the United Empire Loyalists and given grants of land in Nova Scotia, Québec, and Ontario. There is one story that in the period 1783–1793 they constituted ten percent of the marriageable male population of Québec; however, I find this high figure a little difficult to credit in view of the high birth rate of the Québecois and the population of the province at that time.

On their arrival in Canada they joined other German soldiers who had done their military service in Canada without crossing the border. The latter also qualified for the land grants. To further complicate matters, many of these "Canadian" Germans emigrated south to the United States a few years later, and others returned to Europe.

Virginia DeMarce, in her book *German Military Settlers in Canada After the American Revolution*, lists some 2,500 names. A few entries taken at random show the valuable genealogical information she has researched so painstakingly:

ABRAHAM Daniel. Brunswick troops. Born Schorborn, aged 36 years 11 months, discharged in Canada 1783. Marysburgh, Ontario.

DUDLOFF, Gotlieb. Surgeon's mate. Regt. of Specht. Born Erichswalde, Saxony. Aged 28 years 7 months.

RAUCH, Joseph. Brunswick troops. Born Innsbruck. Aged 45. Discharged in Canada 1783.

SCHAEFFER, Andreas. Regiment de Barner. Born Kies, Wurzburg. Aged 29. Discharged Canada 1783.

SCHMIDT, Jacque. Private Corps Company. Hesse-Hanau Infantry. Discharged 1783. Born Bellersdorf. Aged 34.

There is more information to be found in the LDS Church records, in Library and Archives Canada in Ottawa, and in the provincial archives of the three provinces of Ontario, Nova Scotia, and Québec.

THE GERMANS IN CANADA

The number of German settlers in Canada was minute compared with the number in the United States, and settlement was confined to two provinces in the early days—Ontario and Nova Scotia. However, many of the Germans in Canada maintained close family and religious ties with German settlers in Pennsylvania and Maryland, and to discover more about your German ancestors in the United States you may find you need to do some of your research in Canada.

German settlers first entered the province of Ontario (then named Upper Canada) from Pennsylvania in about 1786, but there was no mass movement and during the next twenty-one years only twenty-five families settled in the southwestern area of the province—in what is now the city of Kitchener and the county of Waterloo. Many more followed in 1807 as land in Pennsylvania became too costly and frequent subdivision of farms within families reduced agricultural productivity. A German company was formed in Canada to promote immigration from Pennsylvania, primarily among Mennonites. An option was taken on 60,000 acres in 1803, and the purchase money of $40,000 was raised in the United States, mainly from Pennsylvania's Franklin County. A further 45,000 acres was bought a short time afterwards. In those early days all the Germans in Canada were related to families south of the border.

The settlers came from Franklin, Lancaster, Montgomery, and Bucks counties—particularly the townships of Bedminster, Hillborn, Plumstead, and Tinicum. Many of them were descended from Swiss-German Mennonites. The settlement area in Ontario was an isolated one beyond the districts officially opened by the government, and the Germans lived very self-contained lives. They shared a common language and customs and were bound together by the Mennonite religion. The steady influx from Pennsylvania ended by 1828 but was preceded in the early 1820s by a large number of arrivals—known as "Reichsdeutsche"—coming directly from Germany through the port of Halifax. The other source of German settlement in scattered areas of Canada was that of the Hessians—mercenaries who had served with the British forces during the Revolutionary War. When the British were defeated and the United States created, the Hessians came north into Canada and received grants of land from the British government, mainly along the northern shores of Lake Ontario. However, the major and much more important settlement was in the southwest part of the province of Upper Canada and this we will talk about first, returning later to Nova Scotia.

The German area in Waterloo County was first known as Eby-town—named after an early Mennonite bishop, Benjamin Eby—and later as Sandhills and Berlin. The changes in immigration sources at this time—the early 1820s—led to important changes in the life of the area. The Mennonite farmers soon found themselves in a minority position as the later arrivals were primarily Lutheran and Moravian and were more interested in trade and manufacturing than they were in agriculture. By 1833 the words "Made in Berlin" on manufactured goods demonstrated the industrial growth of the area. It was true that good land could still be bought for two dollars an acre in the townships around Berlin such as Wilmot, Woolwich, and Wellesley, and there was still a steady drift north from Pennsylvania, but it was on a very small scale.

By the mid-1830s immigrants were coming to Berlin from all parts of the German area of Europe—Baden, Bayern (Bavaria), Hessen-Darmstadt, Elsass-Lothringen (Alsace-Lorraine), Holstein, Mecklenburg, Württemberg, and even from the German settlements in the Baltic areas of Estonia, Latvia, and Lithuania. No single religious group was predominant—by 1835 the Lutherans, Moravians, Baptists, and Swedenborgians had churches in the area, and by 1850 the Catholics. By this time more than 12,000 Germans had settled in Upper Canada.

In 1857 the Grand Trunk Railway had reached Berlin and the immigrants landing at Québec were able to travel directly to their destination by train. On one day in that year ninety German immigrants arrived in Berlin and thus increased the population by one percent in one day. Most of these newcomers were from Mecklenburg.

In 1916—in the middle of World War I—it was decided, as the result of a plebiscite, to change the name of Berlin to Kitchener. The new name was a tribute to the memory of a British general who had drowned earlier in the year when a battleship on which he was traveling had been torpedoed by a German submarine.

The German influence in Kitchener, and in Waterloo County, is strong and the history of the founding families is well documented. There are many instances where ancestor-hunters of Pennsylvania-German descent have found out more about their ancestry in Kitchener than in Philadelphia or Harrisburg! There are a great many family histories, both published and in manuscript form, in the Grace Schmidt Room of the

Kitchener Public Library (85 Queen Street North, Kitchener, Ontario N2H 2H1; phone: 519-743-0271; website: www.kpl.org/) and at Conrad Grebel University College in the University of Waterloo (140 Westmount Road North, Waterloo, Ontario N2L 3G6; website: http://grebel.uwaterloo.ca/). The latter has a large collection of Mennonite records but not a great many church registers. It must always be remembered, of course, that the Mennonites practiced adult baptism, as did the Baptists.

There are many Mennonite sects in Ontario that do not deposit their records at the university, and you will have a difficult time in tracing their whereabouts. The Old Order Amish keep their genealogical records in the Amish Heritage Historical Library, RR4 Aylmer, Ontario N5H 2R3, but the following sects retain their records: Old Order Mennonite; Beachy Amish Mennonite; Old Colony Mennonite; Conservative Mennonite; Reformed Mennonite; Church of God in Christ, Mennonite; Evangelical Mennonite Mission; and Mennonite Brethren. However, most of the records of the original group of settlers from Pennsylvania are at the University of Waterloo (see above).

Now let us turn to German settlement in the province of Nova Scotia. There is no connection between settlers there and those in Pennsylvania, except in a few isolated cases. The 3,000 Germans who settled in the province came directly from the German area of Europe, almost entirely by direct passage from the port of Rotterdam in the Netherlands to the port of Halifax, Nova Scotia. Settlement on an organized scale started in the mid-1700s when the British government was encouraging Protestant immigration into Canada. In the main, these Germans came from Baden, Hessen, Württemberg, and Rheinland-Pfalz, plus there were a few Swiss-Germans. Some twelve ships carried immigrants to Nova Scotia in the 1750s, and the passenger lists of ten of them have been researched and published by Terrence Punch, Nova Scotia's leading expert on German immigration into the province. Later in the century there was some settlement by the Hessian mercenaries whom I mentioned earlier.

The Germans in Nova Scotia settled mainly in the area of Lunenberg in 1753, but later moved into other places in this small province. There are a number of books about German settlement in Nova Scotia listed in the Bibliography.

RECORDS IN GERMANY

THE EVANGELICAL CHURCH

The Evangelical Church in Germany (Evangelische Kirche in Deutschland—abbreviated as EKD) is a union of twenty-three Lutheran, Reformed, and United regional churches:

Evangelische Kirche in Deutschland (EKD)
Herrenhäuser Strasse 12
30419 Hanover
E-mail: info@ekd.de
Website: www.ekd.de/

Below are the addresses, phone and fax numbers, and URLs for the various EKD churches.

Evangelische Landeskirche Anhalts
Friedrichstrasse 22, 06844 Dessau
Phone: 011-49-34025260. Fax: 011-49-3402526110
Website: www.landeskirche-anhalts.de/

Evangelische Landeskirche in Baden
Blumenstrasse 1-7, 76133 Karlsruhe
Phone: 011-49-72191750. Fax: 011-49-7219175550
Website: www.ekiba.de/

Evangelisch-Lutherische Kirche in Bayern (Bavaria)
Meiserstrasse 11-13, 80333 Munich (München)
Phone: 011-49-895595552. Fax: 011-49-895595666
Website: www.bayern-evangelisch.de/

Evangelische Kirche in Berlin-Brandenburg-schlesische Oberlausitz
Georgenkirchstrasse 69, 10249 Berlin
Phone: 011-49-3024344290. Fax: 011-49-3024344289
Website: www.ekbo.de/

Evangelisch-Lutherische Landeskirche in Braunschweig (Brunswick)
Dietrich-Bonhoeffer-Strasse 1, 38300 Wolfenbüttel
Phone: 011-49-53318020. Fax: 011-49-5331802707
Website: www.landeskirche-braunschweig.de/

Bremische Evangelische Kirche
Kirchenkanzlei
Franziuseck 2-4, 28199 Bremen
Phone: 011-49-42155970. Fax: 011-49-4215597265
Website: www.kirche-bremen.de/

Evangelisch-Lutherische Landeskirche Hannovers (Hanover)
Rote Reihe 6, 30169 Hannover
Phone: 011-49-51112410. Fax: 011-49-5111241266
Website: www.evlka.de/

Evangelische Kirche in Hessen und Nassau (Hesse and Nassau)
Paulusplatz 1, 64285 Darmstadt
Phone: 011-49-61514050. Fax: 011-49-6151405220
Website: www.ekhn.de/

Evangelische Kirche von Kurhessen-Waldeck
Wilhelmshöher Allee 330, 34131 Kassel
Phone: 011-49-56193780. Fax: 011-49-5619378400
Website: www.ekkw.de/

Lippische Landeskirche
Leopoldstrasse 27, 32756 Detmold
Phone: 011-49-523197660. Fax: 011-49-5231976850
Website: www.lippische-landeskirche.de/

Evangelisch-Lutherische Landeskirche Mecklenburgs
Münzstrasse 8-10, 19055 Schwerin
Phone: 011-49-3855185147. Fax: 011-49-3855185162
Website: www.kirche-mv.de/

Nordelbische Evangelisch-Lutherische Kirche
Dänische Strasse 21-35, 24103 Kiel
Phone: 011-49-43197975. Fax: 011-49-4319797979
Website: www.nordelbien.de/

Evangelisch-Lutherische Kirche in Oldenburg
Philosophenweg 1, 26121 Oldenburg
Phone: 011-49-4417701191. Fax: 011-49-4417701299
Website: www.ev-kirche-oldenburg.com/

Protestantische Landeskirche der Pfalz (Palatinate)
Domplatz 5, 67346 Speyer
Phone: 011-49-62326670. Fax: 011-49-6232667199
Website: www.evpfalz.de/

Pommersche Evangelische Kirche (Pomerania)
Bahnhofstrasse 35/36, 17489 Greifswald
Phone: 011-49-3834854342. Fax: 011-49-3834554799
Website: www.kirche-mv.de/

Evangelisch-reformierte Kirche
Saarstrasse 6, 26789 Leer
Phone: 011-49-191980. Fax: 011-49-19198240
Website: www.reformiert.de/

Evangelische Kirche im Rheinland (Rhineland)
Hans-Böckler Strasse 7, 40476 Düsseldorf
Phone: 011-49-21145620. Fax: 011-49-2114562444
Website: www.ekir.de/

Evangelische Kirche der Kirchenprovinz Sachsen (Saxony)
Am Dom 2, 39104 Magdeburg
Phone: 011-49-39153460. Fax: 011-49-3915346111
Website: www.ekmd-online.de/portal/

Evangelisch-Lutherische Landeskirche Sachsens
Lukasstrasse 6, 01069 Dresden
Phone: 011-49-35146920. Fax: 011-49-3514692109
Website: www.landeskirche-sachsen.de/

Evangelische-Lutherische Landeskirche Schaumburg-Lippe
Herderstrasse 27, 31675 Bückeburg
Phone: 011-49-57229600. Fax: 011-49-572296010
Website: www.ekd.de/schaumburg/index2.html

Evangelisch-Lutherische Kirche in Thüringen (Thuringia)
Dr. Moritz-Mitzenheim-Strasse 2a, 99817 Eisenach
Phone: 011-49-369167899. Fax: 011-49-3691678355
Website: www.ekmd-online.de/portal/

Evangelische Kirche von Westfalen (Westphalia)
Altstädter Kirchplatz 5, 33602 Bielefeld
Phone: 011-49-5215940. Fax: 011-49-521594129
Website: www.ekvw.de/

Evangelische Landeskirche in Württemberg
Augustenstrasse 124, 70197 Stuttgart
Phone: 011-49-7112227658. Fax: 011-49-7112227681
Website: www.elk-wue.de/

As you can see, in the past the Protestant churches in Germany were divided into several sects. If you know your emigrant ancestor from Germany was a member of the Evangelical Church, it will help you in your search if you can discover just which sect he belonged to in the old country.

You will find the various church headquarters staff anxious to be of help to you but you must not ask for the impossible. For example, people have been known to write to the North Elbian Evangelical Lutheran Church to the effect "My great-grandfather was a member of the Evangelical Church and came from somewhere near you. He was born in 1870 or thereabouts. Can you look up the baptism entry in the register?" The North Elbian area covers Schleswig-Holstein, Hamburg, Eutin, and Lübeck. You can imagine how impossible it would be to even start to search.

When you write to a church organization, or a small individual church, please remember to enclose an addressed airmail envelope and at least three International Reply Coupons. I am sorry to have to keep repeating myself on this subject, but if you do not pay the return postage you may not get a reply. In addition, it will not hurt your chances of successful cooperation if you offer, in advance, to pay whatever search fees are required. If the search is an easy one you may not be charged anything.

Finally, if you can, write in German. If you cannot, then at least end your letter with the words "Mit freundlichen Grüssen" ("With friendly greetings").

Churches in East Prussia (Ostpreussen)

Before the invasion of East Prussia by the Red Army, the parish registers and church books (Kirchenbücher) from about 500 parishes were removed to what was then West Berlin. They are in the Evangelical Central Archive in Berlin (Evangelisches Zentralarchiv in Berlin, Bethaniendamm 29, 10997 Berlin; website: www.ezab.de/).

There are some missing and many gaps in the ones that survive, but if your ancestors came from East Prussia and were members of the Evangelical Church, these records may be vital to you. There is no listing of the parishes available, but the archives are planning a book about them.

Although 500 parishes are represented, there are in fact over 6,800 books involved, so you can see that the transfer and saving of these records was a major undertaking that reflects great credit on all the people concerned in this enterprise.

The Family History Library has a collection of microfilmed Lutheran records from Memel and the Memel area covering the period 1614–1944. Several archives, including the archives in Russia for this region, may have received the originals after the filming. I am told that one church book from Memel is in the Lithuanian Central State Archives in Vilnius.

THE CATHOLIC CHURCH

The Catholic Church in Germany is organized in ecclesiastical provinces (each under an archbishop), bishoprics (Bistum), and the local parish (Pfarr). There are twenty-seven church archives. These hold the earlier parish registers, as well as confirmation and communion records, and in many cases, the Family Books (Liber de Statu Animarum). There is no countrywide accepted date for the surrender of early records to the various archives.

The Family Books were first introduced in 1614 and include full details of each family in the parish, together with the names of any servants and the occupation of the head of the family. The books were kept in Latin and German and are more complete in some areas than in others. It was compulsory for the priest to maintain the books up to 1918, but since then it has been quite voluntary. The division of Germany after World War II did not affect the boundaries of the various dioceses, and so the re-unification in 1990 had no effect on ecclesiastical divisions.

The address of the Catholic Church headquarters is as follows:

Sekretariat der Deutschen Bischofskonferenz
Kaiserstrasse 161, 53113 Bonn
Phone: 011-49-2281030. Fax: 011-49-228103299
Website: http://dbk.de/

The addresses of the various Catholic Archives are set out below. It should not be difficult for you to decide to which address you should write. If, for example, your ancestors came from Wanzleben, a gazetteer or a good map in your local library will show you it is near Magdeburg, and the list below will give you the address for that diocese. Generally speaking, you will find that the headquarters of each Bistum are located in the largest city of the area:

Klosterplatz 7, 52062 **Aachen**
Phone: 011-49-2414520. Fax: 011-49-241452496
Website: www.kirche-im-bistum-aachen.de/

Fronhof 4, 86152 **Augsburg**
Phone: 011-49-8213166411. Fax: 011-49-8213166419
Website: www.bistum-augsburg.de/

Regensburger Ring 2, 96047 **Bamberg**
Phone: 011-49-951407470. Fax: 011-49-9514074750
Website: www.eo-bamberg.de/

Niederwallstrasse 8-9, 10117 **Berlin**
Phone: 011-49-30326840. Fax: 011-49-3032684193
Website: www.erzbistumberlin.de/

Käthe-Kollwitz-Ufer 84, 01309 **Dresden**
Phone: 011-49-3513364600. Fax: 011-49-3513364791
Website: www.bistum-dresden-meissen.de/

Leonrodplatz 4, 85072 **Eichstätt**
Phone: 011-49-842150700. Fax: 011-49-842150259
Website: www.bistum-eichstaett.de/

Hermannsplatz 9, 99084 **Erfurt**
Phone: 011-49-36165720. Fax: 011-49-3616572444
Website: www.bistum-erfurt.de/

Zwölfling 16, 45127 **Essen**
Phone: 011-49-20122041. Fax: 011-49-2012204570
Website: www.bistum-essen.de/

Schoferstrasse 2, 79098 **Freiburg**
Phone: 011-49-76121880. Fax: 011-49-7612188505
Website: www.erzbistum-freiburg.de/

Paulustor 5, 36037 **Fulda**
Phone: 011-49-661870. Fax: 011-49-66187578
Website: www.bistum-fulda.de/

Carl-von-Ossietzky-Strasse 41, 02826 **Görlitz**
Phone: 011-49-358147820. Fax: 011-49-3581478212
Website: www.bistum-goerlitz.de/

Danziger Strasse 52 a, 20099 **Hamburg**
Phone: 011-49-4024877221. Fax: 011-49-4024877226
Website: www.erzbistum-hamburg.de/

Domhof 18-21, 31134 **Hildesheim**
Phone: 011-49-51213070. Fax: 011-49-5121307488
Website: www.bistum-hildesheim.de/

Marzellenstrasse 32, 50668 **Köln**
Phone: 011-49-22116420. Fax: 011-49-2211641700
Website: www.erzbistum-koeln.de/

Rossmarkt 4, 65549 **Limburg**
Phone: 011-49-64312950. Fax: 011-49-6431295476
Website: www.bistumlimburg.de/

Max-Josef-Metzger-Strasse 1, 39104 **Magdeburg**
Phone: 011-49-39159610. Fax: 011-49-3915961100
Website: www.bistum-magdeburg.de/

Bischofsplatz 2, 55116 **Mainz**
Phone: 011-49-61312530. Fax: 011-49-6131253401
Website: www.bistummainz.de/

Postfach 33 03 60, 80063 **München**
Phone: 011-49-8921370. Fax: 011-49-8921371585
Website: www.erzbistum-muenchen-und-freising.de/

Domplatz 27, 48143 **Münster**
Phone: 011-49-2514950. Fax: 011-49-2514956086
Website: www.bistummuenster.de/

Kleine Domsfreiheit 23, 49074 **Osnabrück**
Phone: 011-49-541318510. Fax: 011-49-541318117
Website: www.bistum-osnabrueck.de/

Domplatz 3, 33098 **Paderborn**
Phone: 011-49-52511251287. Fax: 011-49-5251125470
Website: www.erzbistum-paderborn.de/

Residenzplatz 8, 94032 **Passau**
Phone: 011-49-8513930. Fax: 011-49-851393830
Website: www.bistum-passau.de/

Niedermünstergasse 1, 93047 **Regensburg***
Phone: 011-49-94159701. Fax: 011-49-9415971055
Website: www.bistum-regensburg.de/

Eugen-Bolz-Platz 1, 72108 **Rottenburg**
Phone: 011-49-74721690. Fax: 011-49-7472169561
Website: www.drs.de/

Kleine Pfaffengasse 16, 67346 **Speyer**
Phone: 011-49-62321020. Fax: 011-49-6232102300
Website: http://cms.bistum-speyer.de/www1/

Hinter dem Dom 6, 54290 **Trier** (Postfach 1340, 54203 Trier)
Phone: 011-49-65171050. Fax: 011-49-6517105498
Website: http://www.bistum-trier.de/

Domerschulstrasse 2, 97070 **Würzburg**
Phone: 011-49-9313861. Fax: 011-49-931386334
Website: www.bistum-wuerzburg.de/

The church registers are either in the original parish church or in one of the church archives listed above. Unfortunately, there is no hard-and-fast rule which says that registers must be sent to the archives on a certain date. In fact, there is no law at all controlling this matter. Even if a church is closed, it is not possible to say with certainty that the registers were then lodged in the church archives. They may have been transferred to the nearest church remaining in operation.

---

*A number of church registers from West Prussia are now in these archives. Detailed information is not available but if your Catholic ancestors came from a known location in West Prussia you should check whether the registers are here.

If you know the exact location of the place from which your ancestor came, you can probably identify the particular archive that may have the registers. If you cannot, then I would write to the Sekretariat and ask them where the registers for that particular church are now.

OTHER RELIGIOUS GROUPS

The two largest of the Protestant free churches, the Methodists and the Evangelical Community (Evangelische-Gemeinschaft), joined in 1968 to form the Evangelical Methodist Church (Evangelisch-Methodistische Kirche; website: www.emk.de/). There is also the Alliance of Free Evangelical Congregations—Baptists (Bund Evangelisch-Freikirchlicher—Baptisten), as well as Mennonites, Quakers, and Jews. By and large, all these organizations leave the registers and other records in the individual churches.

In 1933 there were over half a million Jews living in Germany. In 1990, at the time of German unification, there were approximately thirty thousand Jews living in the merged country. Today there are more than three times as many—due mainly to the influx of Jews who have immigrated to Germany from the former Soviet Union—and the Jewish population continues to grow. The umbrella organization for all Jews in Germany is the Zentralrat der Juden in Deutschland (Central Council of Jews (www.zentralratdjuden.de/). Documents from Jewish communities and organizations are stored at the Central Archives for Research on the History of the Jews in Germany; its address is as follows:

Zentralarchiv zur Erforschung der Geschichte der Juden in Deutschland
Bienenstrasse 5
69117 Heidelberg
Website: www.uni-heidelberg.de/institute/sonst/aj/index.html

THE CALENDAR

Before searching German records, you should be aware of changes in the calendar which, over a period of some years, produced either opposing and contradictory systems, or two different systems existing side by side.

Until 1582 the Julian calendar, established by Julius Caesar, was used in Germany and, indeed, in all civilized countries. This calendar divided the year into 365 days, plus an extra day every fourth year. The system was in operation until 1582, but astronomers had discovered that it exceeded the solar year by eleven minutes—or three days every four hundred years. Between the date when the Julian calendar was established in 325 and the year 1582, the difference amounted to eleven days. Since this affected the calculations for Easter, Pope Gregory XIII decreed that ten days be dropped from the calendar in order to bring Easter to the correct date. To prevent a recurrence of the problem, he also ordered that in every four hundred years leap year's extra day be omitted in a centennial year when the first two digits could not be divided by four without a remainder.

Are you still with me? Well, it means that it was omitted in 1700, 1800, and 1900 but was not omitted in 2000. The Pope also changed the beginning of the New Year from March 25 to January 1, and this new system became known as the Gregorian calendar.

Generally speaking, the new calendar came into force in Germany between 1582 and 1585, depending on the locality. There were some places that started it later and the most important of these are listed below:

Prussia (Preussen)	1612
Pfalz-Neuburg	1615
Osnabrück	1624
Minden	1630
Hildesheim	1631
Friesland	1700

Basically, the Protestant areas were reluctant to make the change, while the Catholic areas started as soon as possible after the papal decree was issued. So you will find places where the Catholic Church accepted the New Year as starting on January 1 and so called September the ninth month, while the Lutheran Church in the same place regarded March 25 as the New Year and regarded September as the seventh month.

When the change did take place, it led to confusing entries of dates in church registers for a brief period. Once the reason is clear to you, you will not be puzzled to find that an ancestress of yours had one child born in one year and a second born a few months later. It was the calendar that changed and not the nine-month gestation period, so all is well!

CHURCH RECORDS

Some church records date back to the fifteenth century, but in fact you should not expect to find many of them before about 1563 for the Catholic Church and a few years later for the Lutherans. Some of the exceptions are to be found in Baden and Württemberg, where there are Lutheran and Catholic registers dating back to the early 1500s.

Although civil registration did not come into force until recent times, very early church registers often contained detailed information about individuals in the parish. Remember, of course, that most church records showed only dates of baptism, marriage, and burial, and you may never find out the dates of birth and death.

Many of the registers have been destroyed as the result of civil wars, rebellions, and invasions over the centuries, but in some cases duplicates were kept in a separate location, so all is not necessarily lost. In Mecklenburg, for example, copies were kept from 1740 onwards.

If you are searching church registers in person, you must be prepared to cope with entries in Latin (until the mid-nineteenth century) and the old German script, plus bad handwriting, and even a style of handwriting that is very different from that of the present day. No one ever said ancestor-hunting was easy!

Illegitimacy was fairly common in some rural areas of Germany. The illegitimate children were always baptized, but often the entry was made upside-down or sideways to emphasize the difference. The entry itself was very specific. The child was a bastard (Hurenkind), the mother a whore (Hure), and the father a fornicator (Hurer) or an adulterer (Ehebrecher).

The entries in the church registers usually include the following information:

BAPTISMS: Name, sex, date, names of parents, father's occupation, place of birth, names and addresses of godparents.

MARRIAGES: Name, age, and address of bride and bridegroom, occupation of groom, names and addresses of parents, occupation of the two fathers.

BURIALS: Name, age, place of death, cause of death, names of parents, name of husband or wife if still alive, date and place of burial.

Usually the above entries were made in three separate registers, but occasionally you will find all three events entered in one register in chronological order as they occurred.

In some parishes, particularly in the eighteenth and nineteenth centuries, you may find Family Books (Familienbücher or Liber de Statu Animarum). These contained complete records of a family and are of great genealogical value. Always check in a particular locality with the Catholic priest or the Lutheran minister as to the existence of a Family Book.

The book showed the name of the head of the household at the time the entry was made, the full names of the various members of the household, their places of birth, their marital status, the dates of death of deceased family members, and the place to which a family member moved if he or she left home (for marriage, work, or emigration). Check also for Kirchenbuchduplikate, a duplicate of entries in the church register which was sent each year to the nearest headquarters of the particular church.

OTHER CHURCH RECORDS

Grave Registers (Grabregister)

These were maintained in the parish church, and although they were a duplicate of the entry of burial in the church register, they often contained additional information such as the date of death and the exact age (i.e., 38 years, 204 days). As the burial entries usually gave the date of *burial* and the age only in years, the grave registers can be of great help.

Church Receipt Books (Einnahmebücher)

These gave details of payments received from church members for such services as bell-tolling for a funeral (with name of deceased and date), and payment for burial plots and funeral cloths (Leichenhemden).

Confirmation Records (Konfirmationbücher)

Most children were between thirteen and twenty when they were confirmed, in both the Catholic and the Lutheran churches. The list gives the child's name and place and date of birth; the name and occupation of the father; and—quite often—the later marriage of the child. These records are either in the original churches or in the church archives.

There is one problem you should consider in connection with church records. If you know the religion of your ancestor but have problems with the location of his or her birthplace because you discover a number of places in Germany with the same name, you may find some help in knowing which religion was predominant in certain areas.

For example, let us suppose you know your Catholic ancestor came from a place named Schwarzenberg. You find there is one place with that name in Hesse (Hessen), one in Brandenburg, one in Prussia (Preussen), and one in Bavaria (Bayern). The odds are that the place you want is in Bavaria, because Brandenburg and Prussia are mainly Lutheran, and Hesse is Protestant but not necessarily Lutheran. This is not an infallible method, but it may help.

The other problem that may cause you difficulty, particularly in Schleswig-Holstein and Friesland, is different naming practices. Farms carried a name, usually the one given to them by the original owner. The name stayed with the farm even when the ownership changed. The trouble is that when a new owner bought the farm he would take its name as his own or, if a man's wife inherited a farm, he would change his name to her maiden name. This could produce the complication of children bearing different surnames within the same family. If you run into this problem, find out if the confirmation books are available for the particular parish, because these records usually give the original name and the later one.

Another naming problem makes life even more difficult. If you see Wilhelm Brode von Magdeburg, for example, in a list, it does not necessarily mean that Wilhelm was a noble. It could simply be that he was a man named Wilhelm Brode who came from Magdeburg. It could be the case that he had moved from Magdeburg to Hannover and found that Brode was a common name, and so to distinguish himself from all the other Wilhelm Brodes he added the words "von Magdeburg." A generation later it could be shortened by his son to Ernst von Magdeburg.

So the surname may, in fact, be your guide to the actual place of origin of the family. Your next problem will be to discover the original surname, and this you may find if you can trace the baptismal or confirmation record of Ernst, because they are likely to give the true surname.

The final naming problem in this particular area is that of the practice of using patronymics—the naming of a child by giving him a new surname based on the first name of the father. Thus Wilhelm, son of Ernst Borgman, could be christened as Wilhelm Ernst. In instances like this, you must again have recourse to baptismal and confirmation records in order to trace the real surname. If you trace an ancestor back to a particular place and find no one of that name in the place before him, then your most obvious reaction is to assume he must have come there from elsewhere. However, do not make this assumption until you have checked out the possibility of a name change.

PASSENGER LISTS

In most countries these are either nonexistent or so few in relation to the whole that they need not be considered as a source of genealogical information. In Germany, however, the story is very different, and that is why I put them second to church registers as a good source of information. In fact, they are equally vital to people whose ancestors came from many other countries in Europe—Austria, Bulgaria, the former Czechoslovakia, Hungary, Poland, Romania, Serbia, the Scandinavian countries, and the former USSR.

Bremen and Hamburg were the main ports for European emigration from 1832 (Bremen) and 1845 (Hamburg) up to 1934. Unfortunately, most of the Bremen lists were destroyed (see page 60 for more information on these lists), but the Hamburg lists from 1850 to 1934 (with the exception of January to June 1853 and August 1914 to 1919) are available online at **www.ancestry.com** (payment required) and on microfilm from the LDS Family History Library. They can also be viewed at a new facility in Hamburg called Port of Dreams–Emigrant World BallinStadt (Veddeler Bogen 2, 20539 Hamburg; phone: 011-49-40-31979160; website: www.ballinstadt.de/), which has special exhibition areas, a public research section with computer workstations for visitors interested in tracing the emigration history of their ancestors, and staff members who are specially trained in genealogy and are available to provide assistance. The passenger lists contain the names of over five million people who emigrated through the port. An index to the Hamburg Passenger Lists for the year 1872 (one of the years with an especially large number of emigrants leaving) is online at **www.progenealogists. com/germany/Hamburg/index.html**.

The State Archives in Hamburg house the original passenger lists of emigrants who sailed overseas directly from Hamburg, or indirectly via Hamburg to other European ports. For example, many emigrants sailed to a British port such as Gravesend or Harwich, crossed the country by train, and then sailed overseas from Liverpool. However, the lists were only compiled for ships with more than twenty-five passengers. They are indexed on a yearly basis in rough alphabetical order. The LDS index is more accurate.

The passenger lists are divided into direct and indirect records. Most emigrants traveled *directly* to a port in their new homeland. For example, the great majority of emigrants to the United States landed in New York; from there they scattered across the country and to Canada and South America.

You will not need to search the lists, of course, if you already know the place of origin of your emigrating ancestor, and the details of his or her family. It will be much easier and less expensive to try other sources first (family stories, diaries, Bibles, naturalization records, or letters).

It is important to realize that not all emigrating Germans used Hamburg or Bremen. Some sailed from Le Havre in France. You must remember, too, that the place of origin shown in the passenger lists is not always the birthplace. However, in that case the odds are that the place of birth was quite near the place of domicile. For example, your ancestor may be shown as coming from Herrenhäusen (a small city), whereas his place of birth may have been Neuburg, a little village a few miles away.

Even if you find no record in the Hamburg lists, all is not lost. Several of the German states kept their own records of emigration from the state, notably Brunswick (Braunschweig), Hesse (Hessen), and Württemberg. Other similar records were kept in many individual cities and towns.

If you are consulting the lists yourself the following glossary may be of help to you:

Alter	Age
Anschrift	Address
Auswanderer	Emigrant
Beruf	Occupation
Bestimmungsort	Destination
Datum	Date
Erwachsen	Adult
Geboren	Born
Geburtsort	Birthplace
Gewerbe	Occupation
Herkunftsort	Place of origin
Kinder	Children
Länder	Provinces or states
Ledig	Single
Namen	Names
Nationalität	Nationality
Ort	Place
Strasse	Street
Verheiratet	Married
Vorname	Given name
Wohin	Destination
Zuname	Surname

Other possible sources of information are the official lists of permits to emigrate. Most of these have been lost, but some have been published for the areas of Brunswick (Braunschweig), Nassau, Sachsen-Weimar, and Waldeck. The German Genealogical Society of America has copies of these.

Another source of information about arrivals in the United States from the Germanic areas of Europe is a multi-volume work called *Germans to America: Lists of Passengers Arriving at U.S. Ports 1850–1891*, ed. Ira A. Glazier and P. William Filby.

In August 2005 a new museum opened on the New Harbor in Bremerhaven where, between 1852 and 1890, almost 1.2 million people left for the New World. The German Emigration Center—the winner of the prestigious European Museum of the Year Award for 2007—contains an extensive library with more than 2,000 volumes on the topic of emigration, as well as a continually growing collection of photographs, biographies, documents, and databases that might help you research ancestors who emigrated to the United States. Here is the contact information:

German Emigration Center
Columbusstrasse 65, 27568 Bremerhaven
Phone: 011-49-471-902200. Fax: 011-49-471-9022022
E-mail: info@dah-bremerhaven.de
Website: www.dah-bremerhaven.de/

Names

In your search of records remember it was common in the middle 1700s in the Germanic areas to use only the *second* baptismal name in official records in later life. The first name was that of a parent or grandparent and was given as a compliment but never used officially. So Oskar Georg Weber would only appear as Georg Weber.

OFFICIAL RECORDS

Civil Registration (Reichspersonenstandsgesetz)

This started in 1875 following the unification of Germany, but only so far as the main Germanic area was concerned. In some areas the system had started earlier. There is a Register Office (Standesamt) for each particular area. All records of births, marriages, and deaths are kept there, but a duplicate of each entry is sent to the state capital. It should be noted that a registration area can be quite large, covering several towns and villages.

In those areas originally under French control, such as Alsace-Lorraine (Elsass-Lothringen) and a few other small areas west of the Rhine, registration started in 1810; in Frankfurt (once a Free City) it began in 1850, in Lübeck and Oldenburg in 1811, in Hanover (Hannover) in 1809, and in most parts of Prussia (Preussen) in about 1870. The death registers are particularly useful because they very often give not only the place and date of death, but also the names of the parents of the deceased and any surviving children.

Wills (Testamente)

The probate system in Germany is a little complicated. Once a lawyer has drawn up a will, a copy is deposited in the district courthouse (Amtsgericht) for the area in which the testator is *living*. The local authorities then notify the Civil Register Office (Standesamt) in the district where the testator was *born*. When he dies, the Standesamt in his place of death notifies the Standesamt in his place of birth, and the latter, in turn, notifies the Court of Law of the location of the will. The court then executes the will. Original wills are either in the district courthouse or in the state archives (Staatsarchiv) in each province.

Censuses (Volkszählungen)

These have been held on a countrywide basis since 1871, with the first large-scale census taking place in 1895, but others were held at irregular intervals in various areas. However, many censuses did not survive World War II, and generally only the compiled statistical information that was gathered from the censuses is available, so they are not of great use to genealogists. Census records of some provinces or towns may be accessible at various archives, but you'd have to hunt around to find ones that are available to researchers. Check with the municipal archives (Stadtarchiv) or the Civil Register Office (Standesamt) in each city or district to see if any records are available. East Germany, when it was independent, destroyed its census returns after counting.

GERMANY: 1871, 1880, 1885, 1890, 1895, 1900, 1905, 1910, 1919, 1925, 1933, 1939

WEST GERMANY: 1946, 1950, 1961, 1970, 1987

EAST GERMANY: 1946, 1964, 1971, 1981

BADEN: 1852, 1855, 1858, 1861, 1867, 1925, 1933, 1946

BADEN-WÜRTTEMBERG: 1946, 1950, 1961, 1970

BAYERN (BAVARIA): 1846, 1849, 1852, 1855, 1858, 1861, 1867, 1946, 1950, 1961, 1970

BERLIN (WEST): 1945, 1946, 1950, 1961, 1970

BERLIN (EAST): 1945, 1946, 1964

BREMEN: 1900, 1905, 1946, 1950, 1961, 1970

DRESDEN: 1871

HAMBURG: 1866, 1867, 1871, 1946, 1950, 1961, 1970

HESSEN (HESSE): 1925, 1946, 1950, 1961, 1970

KÖLN (COLOGNE): 1961

NORDRHEIN-WESTFALEN (NORTH RHINE-WESTPHALIA): 1946, 1950, 1961, 1970

PREUSSEN (PRUSSIA): 1895, 1900, 1905, 1910

RHEINLAND-PFALZ (RHINELAND-PALATINATE): 1946, 1950, 1961, 1970

SAARLAND: 1927, 1935, 1961, 1970 (see under France for 1945–57)

SCHLESWIG-HOLSTEIN: 1803, 1835, 1840, 1855, 1860, 1946, 1950, 1961, 1970

WÜRTTEMBERG: 1821, 1832, 1843, 1846, 1849, 1852, 1855, 1858, 1861, 1867, 1946, 1950

DEUTSCHER ZOLLVEREIN: 1855 (This was the area included in a Customs Union of North German States.)

The census returns of several areas have been copied by the LDS Church and are available at the Family History Library. The 1819 census of Mecklenburg-Schwerin is one of the most significant at the library, since the complete census survived and information in the census includes name, gender, birth date, place of birth, marital status, occupation, and religion. Various census records for Schleswig-Holstein are also among those available at the library.

Police Registration (Einwohnermelderegister)

This started in most of the states about 1840 and controlled internal movement. The records included full name, family details, date and place of birth, and occupation. As I mentioned earlier in this chapter, the records are usually held in local archives, police headquarters, or state archives.

Military Records (Kriegslisten)

These are incomplete and not always easily accessible but they are worth working on because every male was liable for military service in the various state armies. If your ancestors came from the Schleswig-Holstein area, you are luckier than most. The system there involved the registration of every male child at birth, and the record was kept up-to-date as far as addresses were concerned until his call-up date. A good sequence of discoveries can follow: if you find your ancestor's addresses from the military records, you can trace the census returns; if you find the census returns you find the place of birth; if you find the place of birth you find the church records, you lucky people from Schleswig-Holstein! The military lists in general date back to the early 1700s and are in the state archives.

Certificate of Birth (Geburtszeugnis or Geburtsbrief)

When a person wanted to establish citizenship in a city or town, or get married, or join a guild (see below), he or she would have to produce this document. The individual had to produce a letter from the priest or pastor in his or her birthplace and the civil authorities would then issue the certificate.

Guild Records (Gilderbücher)

These can provide valuable information for you. The guild (like the trade union of today) was powerful in the work field. It permitted its members to work only at a particular trade, in a particular place. It made sure that a newcomer in town became a citizen before he joined the guild. Remember that being an inhabitant was not the same as being a citizen. Anyone could be an inhabitant, but you had to earn the right to become a citizen. You had to work hard, not be a charge on the community, not be a bastard, be sober, be a churchgoer, and know the right people.

Then, and only then, the good citizen could apply to join a guild, and the guild records show his name, his trade, the names of his wife and children, the date and place of his birth, the date and place of his marriage, and the date of his arrival in the city and his entry into the guild. The guilds exercised so much control over their members that they could dictate the area of the city in which they lived, and even whom they married (preferably the daughter of another guild member).

The guild records are either in local archives or in state archives, and they date back in many cases to the early seventeenth century, and in a few instances even earlier.

Other Available Records

There are three important sources of information in Germany that are often overlooked. They are, in order of value, Ortssippenbücher (Local Family Books), Geschlechterbücher (Lineage Books), and Leichenpredigten (Funeral Sermons).

These records should be used in conjunction with all the other sources I have listed; none of them, on their own, will provide you with all the answers, but they may well fill gaps, solve relationship puzzles, and give you the place of origin, marriage, or death of a particular ancestor. Unfortunately, the records I mention are not in any one place, nor are the locations listed. You will have to write to the particular place or general area in which you are interested: to the Mayor (Bürgermeister) for a village, town, or city; or to the local Catholic priest or Lutheran minister; or to the director of the city archives (Stadtsarchiv) or the provincial archives (Landesarchiv or Staatsarchiv). You will have to ferret out the locations for yourself, but I never promised you a Rosengarten!

Local Family Books (Ortssippenbücher)

German genealogists and sociologists have been very interested since the early part of this century in studying the various families living in a particular area. This is partly pure research, partly love of history, and partly the German passion for tidiness, for having everything in its proper place. The Ortssippenbuch for a particular area will list all the members of every family (living and dead) and their relationship with each other. The source of the information was, of course, the church register, both Lutheran and Catholic.

As interest in the projects grew, the organization of them was taken over by a branch of the government, and as each district was completed, the results were published in book form. The ultimate aim was to have a genealogical record of the entire German people.

This was a point where the interests of genealogists in tracing family descent coincided with the National Socialist racial policies for a brief period. After 1933 many German citizens, particularly farmers, store-owners, and teachers, were required to provide a certificate proving their Aryan descent—der Ahnennachweis, as it was called—and the existence of a completed Ortssippenbuch for their district simplified their task. The tracing of lineage was required back to the early nineteenth century; only the S.S. demanded lineage back to 1750 for their members.

Publication was suspended in 1940; after the war the task was taken over by the genealogical organizations without regard to any racial purity, and today some 150 books are in print. In addition, very many books were started and never finished, or finished and never printed. You will find the books or manuscripts in local and state archives. The present-day compiling of the books is not being done on a very even basis, since it depends very much on the energy and dedication of the various genealogical organizations. About half of the completed books refer to districts in the Länder of Baden and Hessen-Nassau.

It should be mentioned that some manuscripts are still in the possession of the individuals who worked on them, and if you are referred to a private individual, your approach should be a tactful one, since not everyone wishes to be reminded of the original reasons for their genealogical research.

A list compiled in 1997 of existing Ortssippenbucher is available online at **www.genealogienetz.de/faqs/ortsbuch**.

German Lineage Books (Deutsche Geschlechterbücher)

These books date back in some cases to the late eighteenth century when the first known one was published. The contents, of course, go back very much further. They contain the details of descent of bourgeois families, i.e. middle class and lower upper class, not the nobility. Each book contains a number of family trees of various German families. They are on a regional basis in that all the families in the book are from one district.

Some 200 of the Geschlechterbücher have been published, and more are on the way. Each family section starts with the earliest known member and descends through the years to the date of publication. It also lists occupations, and places of baptism, marriage, death, and residence.

The LDS Family History Library has all but a few volumes in its collection. These volumes often give many generations of German families. They are indexed at the end of each volume, and the first 150 volumes are indexed in a cumulative index called *Stammfolgen-Verzeichnisse für das genealogische Handbuch des Adels und das deutsche Geschlechterbuch*, which is also available at the Family History Library, as is a filmed copy of the 1963 index for volumes 1–134.

Funeral Sermons (Leichenpredigten)

This source of genealogical information is almost unique to Germany but I have found similar records in Hungary. They originated in the sixteenth century for a rather odd reason. When the Reformation reached Germany it meant the end of a very ornate and impressive funeral mass in the Catholic Church. This was a great occasion in which the deceased was praised at length by a local orator (often a professional, paid for his services), a large choir performed, and a sermon was delivered by the local priest (or by the bishop if the dead man or woman was important enough, or if the remaining spouse was generous to the church).

The end of this kind of ceremony left a gap in the lives of many people, mainly among Lutherans and Calvinists. They had embraced a simple and stark religion, but many of them missed a good funeral mass! So the funeral sermon was born and took the form of a eulogy at the graveside. Some sermons were entirely religious in content, but many were biographical and recounted the whole life of the deceased with details of births, marriages, public or military service, and other events of note.

After the ceremony the sermons were printed and circulated to all the friends of the family. There are well over 100,000 of these preserved in various locations and covering the period from about 1550 up to around 1800. Some of them are only a page or two in length, but some, if the deceased was famous, run to a hundred pages or more!

You can usually depend on the information contained in them being accurate; since the sermon was to be circulated among family and friends there was no point in lying or exaggerating the life and accomplishments of the deceased. Obviously, certain events would probably be quietly ignored: a period of insanity, a bastard child, dishonorable discharge from the army, a conviction for theft—that sort of thing would be left unsaid.

You can see that these three sources may well be of great value to you. Remember, though, that two of them are limited in their scope. The Lineage Books are confined to the bourgeois families, the Funeral Sermons to the wealthier Protestants, and only the local Family Books record everybody, Catholic and Lutheran, rich and poor, in fact all classes of society.

Because the records I have mentioned are scattered in so many municipal offices, libraries, and archives, the search for one that includes your own family may be long-drawn-out, but if you are successful you may find your family lineage for a good many years, even two or three centuries.

There are still more available records of use to you. In some localities you will find all of them, in others only one or two:

	Approximate starting date
Adressbuch (City Directory)	1750*
Bürgerbuch (Citizenship Record)	1300
Familienregister (Family Registers)	1800
Gerichtsprotokolle (Court Records)	1500*
Grundbücher (Land Records)	1000*
Lehrlingsbücher (Apprentice Records)	1550
Polizeiregister (Police Registers)	1800
Stadtchroniken (City Chronicles)	1600
Steuerbücher (Tax Records)	1400
Zeitungen (Newspapers)	1800*

The dates are approximate because they vary from province to province, and from city to city. Generally speaking, the records marked with an asterisk are in the provincial archives (Staats- und Landesarchiv) and the others in city archives (Stadtarchiv) or district archives (Kreisarchiv), but there are exceptions to this.

One of the major problems about German records of interest to the ancestor-hunter is that they are scattered among church archives, state archives, city, town, and village archives, some government departments and offices, libraries, and museums. To make matters worse, only one attempt has been made to list the location of all genealogical archives and that effort, though praiseworthy, is very incomplete. Make no mistake: the material is there; it is available and informative; and it goes back over the centuries. Even minor local events were recorded and will be of interest to you. Many records are available on microfilm through the LDS Church. Take a look at the various links for German research information on the LDS website at **www.familysearch.org** and review the LDS *Germany Research Outline* at **www.familysearch. org/Eng/Search/rg/guide/Germany29.asp** to see what information is available through them.

ARCHIVES

The many divisions of the Germanic area are the cause of the peculiar distribution of archives. From the fourteenth to the nineteenth century, central power over the Germanic lands was exercised by the Hapsburg dynasty, so the central archives of the old Reich are in Vienna (Wien).

Since then, the various states have preserved their own archives; as a result, there are archives of all kinds scattered throughout Germany, from major cities down to small villages, and there are no central archives with precious genealogical records.

You will find Staatsarchiv (national), Staatsarchiv (provincial), Landesarchiv (provincial), Stadt (city), Bezirk (district), Dorf (village), Familien (family), Dom (cathedral), Pfarr (parish), Gutsarchiv (property), plus many others for individuals, families, professions, manufacturing plants, religious orders, and youth organizations.

In the following pages you will find details of many of the archives of value to the ancestor-hunter: first, the provincial or state archives; then a list of local archives alphabetically by city, town, and village; finally a list of church archives at a level lower than those included earlier in this chapter. In addition you will find a list of archives devoted to the papers of noble families.

State and Provincial Archives

Landesarchiv Baden-Württemberg
Eugenstrasse 7
70182 Stuttgart
Phone: 011-49-7112124272; Fax: 011-49-7112124283
E-mail: landesarchiv@la-bw.de
Website: www.landesarchiv-bw.de/

Hauptstaatsarchiv Stuttgart
Konrad-Adenauer-Strasse 4
70173 Stuttgart
Phone: 011-49-7112124335. Fax: 011-49-7112124360
E-mail: hstastuttgart@la-bw.de
Website: www.landesarchiv-bw.de/

Bayerisches Hauptstaatsarchiv
Schönfeldstrasse 5-11
80539 Munich
Phone: 011-49-89286382482. Fax: 011-49-89286382615
E-mail: poststelle@gda.bayern.de
Website: www.gda.bayern.de/

Landesarchiv Berlin
Eichborndamm 115-121
13403 Berlin
Phone: 011-49-30902640. Fax: 011-49-3090264201
E-mail: info@landesarchiv-berlin.de
Website: www.landesarchiv-berlin.de/

Brandenburgisches Landeshauptarchiv
An der Orangerie 3
Postfach 600409

14404 Potsdam
Phone: 011-49-33156740. Fax: 011-49-3315674112
E-mail: poststelle@blha.brandenburg.de
Website: www.landeshauptarchiv-brandenburg.de/

Staatsarchiv Bremen
Am Staatsarchiv 1
28203 Bremen
Phone: 011-49-4213616221. Fax: 011-49-42136110247
E-mail: zentrale@staatsarchiv.bremen.de
Website: www.staatsarchiv.bremen.de/

Staatsarchiv Hamburg
Kattunbleiche 19
22041 Hamburg
Phone: 011-49-40428313200. Fax: 011-49-428313201
Website: www.staatsarchiv.hamburg.de/

Hessisches Hauptstaatsarchiv
Mosbacher Strasse 55
65187 Wiesbaden
Phone: 011-49-6118810. Fax: 011-49-611881145
E-mail: Poststelle@hhstaw.hessen.de
Website: www.hauptstaatsarchiv.hessen.de/

Landeshauptarchiv Schwerin
Graf-Schack-Allee 2
19053 Schwerin
Phone: 011-49-385592960. Fax: 011-49-3855929612
E-mail: poststelle@landeshauptarchiv-schwerin.de
Website: www.landeshauptarchiv-schwerin.de/

Niedersächsisches Hauptstaatsarchiv
Am Archiv 1
30169 Hannover
Phone: 011-49-5111206601. Fax: 011-49-5111206639
E-mail: poststelle@nla.niedersachsen.de
Website: www.staatsarchive.niedersachsen.de/

Landesarchiv Nordrhein-Westfälisches Hauptstaatsarchiv Düsseldorf
Mauer Strasse 55
40476 Düsseldorf
Phone: 011-49-211220650. Fax: 011-49-2112206555501
E-mail: has@lav.nrw.de/
Website: www.archive.nrw.de/LandesarchivNRW/Duesseldorf/index.
html

Landeshauptarchiv Rheinland-Pfalz
Karmeliterstrasse 1-3
56068 Koblenz
Phone: 011-49-26191290. Fax: 011-49-2619129112
E-mail: post@landeshauptarchiv-ko.de
Website: www.landeshauptarchiv.de/

Landesarchiv Saarbrücken
Dudweilerstrasse 1
66133 Saarbrücken-Scheidt
Phone: 011-49-681980390. Fax: 011-49-68198039133
E-mail: landesarchiv@landesarchiv.saarland.de
Website: www.saarland.de/landesarchiv.htm

Sächsisches Hauptstaatsarchiv Dresden
Archivstrasse 14
01097 Dresden
Phone: 011-49-35180060. Fax: 011-49-3518021274
E-mail: poststelle-d@sta.smi.sachsen.de
Website: www.sachsen.de/archiv

Landeshauptarchiv Sachsen-Anhalt
Hegelstrasse 25
39104 Magdeburg
Phone: 011-49-39156643. Fax: 011-49-3915664440
E-mail: poststelle@lha.mi.lsa-net.de
Website: www.staatsarchive.de/archive/bl14.html

Landesarchiv Schleswig-Holstein
Prinzenpalais
24837 Schleswig
Phone 011-49-4621861800. Fax: 011-49-4621861801
E-mail: landesarchiv@la.landsh.de
Website: www.landesarchiv.schleswig-holstein.de/

Thüringisches Hauptstaatsarchiv Weimar
Marstallstrasse 2
(Postfach 726, 99408 Weimar)
99423 Weimar
Phone: 011-49-36438700. Fax 011-49-364870100
Website: www.thueringen.de/de/staatsarchive/weimar/content.html

Central Office for Genealogy
(Zentralstelle für Genealogie)

The Zentralstelle für Genealogie (Z.G.) was founded as an archive for
genealogical materials, and houses many records from the area once
known as "East Germany." It is part of the National Archive system

of Germany and is located in the Sachsen (Saxony) State Archives, Schongauer Strasse 1, 04329 Leipzig (phone: 011-49-341-2555551; fax: 011-49-341-2555555; website: www.leipzig.de/de/buerger/bildung). The LDS Family History Library has microfilmed many of the archive's records, including an extensive collection of German church records, and records of German settlements in Eastern Europe.

The various holdings include the following:

1. A pedigree and ancestor list which includes more than 12,000 family trees, including over two million card-indexes of individual names. If you are consulting these cards in person (and you may obtain permission to do so), you must know the system. Because of the variation in the spelling of surnames, it was decided to follow a system of phonetic spelling and file under one spelling variation only. So, for example, under the name Maier you will also find Mayer, Meier, and Meyer.

2. A catalogue of personal writings and eulogies. This covers the sixteenth to eighteenth centuries and consists of some 700 works. It is being added to on a regular basis and is certainly only in its infancy, and it includes many printed funeral orations and sermons (I have referred to this German custom earlier).

3. The Z.G. also contains photocopies and microfilms of a number of church registers of all denominations. There is no list available, but this is understandable because the additions are being made constantly and any list would soon be out-of-date.

4. There are more specialized items in the Z.G. records such as the following:

    (a) A list of the population of Leipzig before 1800, including the surrounding area.

    (b) Records of the Huguenots who fled from France after the bloody persecution that followed the revocation of the Edict of Nantes in 1685.

5. The library of Z.G. includes 22,000 writings on genealogical subjects, in both published and manuscript form, covering the period from the seventeenth century to the present.

City Archives (Stadtarchiv)

The type of record you will find in local archives includes all or some of the following. It is up to you to write and find out what is available for your particular district. Try to write in German, because even though there may be someone there who understands English, he or she may not read it well enough to understand just what you want to know. I once wrote and asked for the correct name of a book about leading families in a particular city. I had a reply in flawless English telling me they had only one copy of the book, and in any case it would be too heavy to send through the mail! They did not mention the name of the book, either, so I had to write again in German, and then all was well. You may also find that when you write in English you will be answered in German. In this case you can try to find someone who speaks German, a friend or a local teacher, or settle down with a good German-English dictionary in the local library.

At this point let me again remind you when you use "snail mail" to enclose a self-addressed airmail envelope and three International Reply Coupons to cover return postage. If you are planning a great deal of correspondence with Germany, it will save money if you buy German stamps. Write to the post office (Postamt) of any German city, enclose a bank draft for a sum of money (five or ten dollars), and ask them to mail you German stamps of the right value for airmail letters to this country.

The type of records you will find are listed below:

Address Books (Adressbücher)
Apprentice Lists (Lehrlingsbücher)
Census Returns (Volkszählungen)
City Chronicles (Stadtchroniken)
City Directories (Adressbücher)
Citizenship Lists (Bürgerbücher)
Court Records (Gerichtsprotokolle)
Emigration Lists (Auswanderungregister)
Family Books (Ortssippenbücher)
Family Registers (Familienregister)
Funeral Sermons (Leichenpredigten)
Grave Registers (Grabregister)
Guild Books (Gilderbücher)
Land Records (Grundbücher)
Lineage Books (Geschlechterbücher)
Newspapers (Zeitungen)
Parish Registers (Kirchenbücher)
Police Registers (Polizeiregister)
Probate Records (Testamente)
Tax Records (Steuerbücher)
Wills (Testamente)

The following abbreviations are used in the list of cities, towns, etc., to show the provinces or Länder in which the places are located:

BW	Baden-Württemberg
B	Bayern
BL	Bremen
BR	Brandenburg

H	Hessen
HL	Hamburg
MV	Mecklenburg-Vorpommern
NS	Niedersachsen
NW	Nordrhein-Westfalen
RP	Rheinland-Pfalz
S	Saarland
SA	Sachsen
SAA	Sachsen-Anhalt
SH	Schleswig-Holstein
T	Thüringen

Aachen (NW)
Aalen (BW)
Abensberg (B)
Ahaus (NW)
Ahrweiler (RP)
Alsfeld (H)
Altdorf (B)
Altena (NW)
Altenburg (SA)
Alt-Wallmoden (NS)
Alzey (RP)
Amlishagen (BW)
Amöneburg (H)
Amstetten (B)
Andernach (RP)
Anklam (MV)
Annaberg-Buckholz
　(SA)
Annweiler (RP)
Ansbach (B)
Apolda (T)
Arnsberg (NW)
Arnstadt (T)
Artern (SAA)
Aschaffenburg (B)
Ascherleben (T)
Aue (SA)
Augsburg (B)
Babenhausen (H)
Bacharach (RP)
Backnang (BW)

Balingen (BW)
Bamberg (B)
Baunatal (H)
Bayreuth (B)
Beeskow (BR)
Bensheim (H)
Bentheim (NS)
Bergisch-Gladbach
　(NW)
Bad Bergzabern (RP)
Berleburg (NW)
Berlin
Bernburg (SAA)
Besighem (BW)
Bevensen (NS)
Biberach (BW)
Bielefeld (NW)
Bingen (RP)
Bischofswerda (SA)
Bitterfeld (SAA)
Blaubeuren (BW)
Blomberg (NW)
Bocholt (NW)
Bochum (NW)
Bonn (NW)
Borken (NW)
Borna (SA)
Bottrop (NW)
Flecken Bovenden
　(NS)
Brafkenheim (BW)

Brakel (NW)
Brandenburg an der
　Havel (BR)
Brandestein bei Elm
　(H)
Braunschweig (NS)
Breckerfeld (NW)
Breisach (BW)
Bremen (BL)
Bremerhaven (BL)
Brilon (NW)
Brühl (NW)
Bad Buchau (BW)
Bühl (BW)
Büren (NW)
Burg auf Fehmarn
　(SH)
Burg bei Magdeburg
　(SAA)
Burgbernheime (B)
Burghausen (B)
Burgkunstadt (B)
Burgsteinfurt (NW)
Burkheim am K
　(BW)
Butzbach (H)
Buxtehude (NS)
Calbe (SAA)
Calw (BW)
Castrop-Rauxel
　(NW)

Celle (NS)
Cham (B)
Chemnitz (SA)
Coburg (B)
Coesfeld (NW)
Coswig (SAA)
Cottbus (BR)
Crimmitschau (SA)
Cuxhaven (NS)
Darmstadt (H)
Deggendorf (B)
Deidesheim (RP)
Delitzch (SA)
Demmin (BR)
Dessau (SAA)
Detmold (NW)
Diez (RP)
Dillingen/Donau (B)
Dingolfing (B)
Dinkelsbühl (B)
Dinslaken (NW)
Doberlug-Kirchhain
   (BR)
Donauwörth (B)
Dornburg/Elbe
   (SAA)
Dorsten (NW)
Dortmund (NW)
Dreieichenhain (H)
Dresden (SA)
Dubeln (SA)
Duderstadt (NS)
Duisburg (NW)
Dulmen (NW)
Düren (NW)
Bad Durkheim (RP)
Düsseldorf (NW)
Eberbach (BW)
Eberswalde (BR)
Ebingen (BW)
Eckernförde (SH)
Edenkoben (RP)
Eggenfelden (B)

Eichstatt (B)
Eilenburg (SA)
Einbeck (NS)
Eisenach (T)
Eisenberg (RP)
Eisenberg (T)
Eisfeld (T)
Eisleben (SAA)
Ellwangen (BW)
Emden (NS)
Emmerich (NW)
Bad Ems (RP)
Endingen (BW)
Engen (BW)
Erding (B)
Erfurt (T)
Erkelenz (NW)
Erlangen (B)
Eschwege (H)
Esslingen/Neckar
   (BW)
Eutin (SH)
Feuchtwangen (B)
Flensburg (SH)
Forchheim (B)
Forst/Lausitz (BR)
Bad Frankenhausen
   (SAA)
Frankenthal (RP)
Frankfurt/Main (H)
Frankfurt/Oder (BR)
Frechen (NW)
Freiberg (SA)
Freiburg/Breisgau
   (BW)
Freising (B)
Freudenstadt (BW)
Friedberg/Hessen (H)
Friedrichshafen
   (BW)
Fritzlar (H)
Fulda (H)
Furstenau (NS)

Furstenwalde (BR)
Fürth (B)
Füssen (B)
Gaildorf (BW)
Gardelegen (SAA)
Garmisch/
   Partenkirchen (B)
Geinhausen (H)
Geislingen (BW)
Gelsenkirchen (NW)
Gengenbach (BW)
Gera (T)
Gernrode (SAA)
Gerolzhofen (B)
Geseke (NW)
Gevelsberg (NW)
Giengen (BW)
Giessen (H)
Glücksburg (SH)
Glückstadt (SH)
Gnandstein (SA)
Göppingen (BW)
Görlitz (SA)
Goslar (NS)
Gotha (T)
Göttingen (NS)
Greifswald (MV)
Greiz (T)
Greussen (T)
Grimma (SA)
Groitzscg (SA)
Grossbottwar (BW)
Gross-Gerau (B)
Grünberg (H)
Grunstadt (RP)
Guben (BR)
Gudensberg (H)
Güstrow (MV)
Hachenburg (RP)
Hagen (NW)
Halberstadt (SAA)
Halle an der Saale
   (SAA)

Hamburg (HL)	Kaiserlautern (RP)	Lauf (B)
Hameln (NS)	Kalkar (NW)	Laufen (B)
Hanau (H)	Kamenz (SA)	Lauingen/Donau (B)
Hann/Munden (NS)	Kandel (RP)	Lauterbach (H)
Hannover (NS)	Karlshafen (H)	Lauterecken (RP)
Haslach (BW)	Karlsruhe (BW)	Leipzig (SA)
Hattingen (NW)	Karlstadt (B)	Lemgo (NW)
Heidelberg (BW)	Kassel (H)	Leutkirch (BW)
Heidenheim/Brenz	Kaufbeuren (B)	Leverkusen (NW)
(BW)	Kelheim (B)	Lich (H)
Heilbad	Kempen (NW)	Lichtenfels (B)
Heiligenstadt (T)	Kempten/Aligäu (B)	Limburg/Lahn (H)
Helmstedt (NS)	Kenzingen (BW)	Lindau (B)
Herberg/Elster (BR)	Kiel (SH)	Linz (RP)
Herford (NW)	Kirchheim/Teck	Lippstadt (NW)
Herne (NW)	(BW)	Löbau (SA)
Herrenberg (BW)	Kirn (RP)	Lörrach (BW)
Hersbruck (B)	Kirtorf (H)	Lubben (BR)
Bad Hersfeld (H)	Kitzingen (B)	Lübeck (SH)
Herten (NW)	Kleve (NW)	Luckenwalde (BR)
Hildburghausen (T)	Koblenz (RP)	Lüdenscheid (NW)
Hilden (NW)	Köln (NW)	Ludwigsburg (BW)
Hildesheim (NS)	Königshofen (B)	Ludwigshafen (RP)
Hochstadt (B)	Konstanz (BW)	Ludwigslust (MV)
Hof (B)	Korbach/Edersee (H)	Lügde (NW)
Hofgeismar (B)	Köthen/Anhalt	Lüneburg (NS)
Homberg (H)	(SAA)	Lünen (NW)
Bad Homberg (H)	Kranenburg (NW)	Magdeburg (SAA)
Horb/Neckar (BW)	Krefeld (NW)	Mainz (RP)
Hornburg (NS)	Bad Kreuznach (RP)	Mannheim (BW)
Höxter (NW)	Kronach (B)	Marburg (H)
Hüfingen (BW)	Krönberg (H)	Marienberg (SA)
Husum (SH)	Kulmbach (B)	Markdorf (BW)
Ilmenau (T)	Kusel (RP)	Markleeberg (SA)
Ingelheim (RP)	Lage-Lippe (NW)	Marktredwitz (B)
Ingoldstadt (B)	Lahnstein (RP)	Marl (NW)
Iserlohn (NW)	Lahr (BW)	Maulbronn (BW)
Isny (BW)	Landau (RP)	Mayen (RP)
Itzehoe (SH)	Landsberg (B)	Meckenheim (NW)
Jena (T)	Landshut (B)	Meersburg (BW)
Jever (NS)	Bad Langensalza (T)	Meiningen (T)
Jülich (NW)	Laubach (H)	Meisenheim (RP)
Juterbog (BR)	Lauenburg/Elbe (SH)	Meissen (SA)

Meldorf (SH)
Melle (NS)
Memmingen (B)
Menden (NW)
Mengen (BW)
Meppen (NS)
Bad Mergentheim
  (BW)
Merseburg (SAA)
Messkirch (BW)
Metelen (NW)
Mettmann (NW)
Meuselwitz (SA)
Michelstadt (H)
Mindelheim (B)
Minden (NW)
Mittweida (SA)
Moers (NW)
Möhringen (BW)
Mönchengladbach
  (NW)
Monschau (NW)
Montabour (RP)
Mühldorf (B)
Mühlhausen/Thur (T)
München (B)
Münnerstadt (B)
Münster (NW)
Bad Münstereifel
  (NW)
Namedy (RP)
Nassau (RP)
Nauheim (H)
Naumburg/Saale
  (SAA)
Neckarsteinach (H)
Neheim/Hüsten
  (NW)
Neuburg (B)
Neuenburg (BW)
Neuenhaus (NS)
Neumünster (SH)
Neuötting (B)

Neuss (NW)
Neustadt (B)
Neustadt/Donau (B)
Nidda (H)
Nideggen (NW)
Nordhausen (T)
Nordhorn (NS)
Nordlingen (B)
Northeim (NS)
Nürnberg (B)
Nürtingen (BW)
Oberhausen (NW)
Obernburg/Main (B)
Oberndorf (BW)
Oberursel/Taunas (H)
Oberviechtach (B)
Ochsenfurt (B)
Oelsnitz im Vogtland
  (SA)
Offenbach/Main (H)
Offenburg (BW)
Ohrdruf (T)
Ohringen (BW)
Oldenburg (SH)
Oldenburg (NS)
Bad Oldesloe (SH)
Olpe (NW)
Opladen (NW)
Oppenheim (RP)
Oranienburg (BR)
Oschatz (SA)
Oschersleben (SAA)
Osnabrück (NS)
Osterburg (SAA)
Osterrode/Harz (NS)
Otterberg (RP)
Otterndorf (NS)
Paderborn (NW)
Paschim (MV)
Pegau (SA)
Perleberg (MV)
Pforzheim (BW)
Pfullendorf (BW)

Pfullingen (BW)
Pirna (SA)
Plauen im Vogtland
  (SA)
Porz (NW)
Pössneck (T)
Prenzlau (MV)
Pritzwalk (BR)
Bad Pyrmont (NS)
Quakenbrück (NS)
Quedlinnburg (SAA)
Radolfzell (BW)
Rain (B)
Rastatt (BW)
Ratingen (NW)
Ratzeburg (SH)
Ravensburg (BW)
Rees (NW)
Regensburg (B)
Reichenbach im
  Vogtland (SA)
Reinheim (H)
Remagen (RP)
Remscheid (MW)
Rendsburg (SH)
Reutlingen (BW)
Rheda/Wiedenbrück
  (NW)
Rheinberg (NW)
Rheine (NW)
Rhein Hausen (NW)
Rheydt (NW)
Rhoden (H)
Riedlingen (BW)
Rieneck (B)
Riesa (SA)
Rinteln (NS)
Rochlitz (SA)
Romrod (H)
Rosberg (NW)
Rosenheim (B)
Rostock (MV)
Rotenburg (NS)

Roth (B)
Rothernburg (B)
Rottweil (BW)
Rudolstadt (T)
Ruhla (T)
Rüthen (NW)
Saalfeld (T)
Saarbrücken (S)
Saarlouis (S)
St. Goar (RP)
St. Ingbert (S)
Salzgitter (NS)
Bad Salzuflen (NW)
Bad Salzungen (T)
Salzwedel (SAA)
Sangerhausen (SAA)
Schalkau (SAA)
Schleiz (T)
Schleswig (SH)
Schleusingen (T)
Schlitz (H)
Schmalkalden (T)
Schmölin (SA)
Schneeberg (SA)
Schönebeck (SAA)
Schongau (B)
Schopfheim (BW)
Schorndorf (BW)
Schotten (H)
Schramberg (BW)
Schwabach (B)
Schwäbisch Gmünd
  (BW)
Schwäbisch Hall
  (BW)
Schweinfurt (B)
Schwelm (NW)
Schwerin (MV)
Schwetzingen (BW)
Seefeld (B)
Seehausen/Altmark
  (SAA)
Seligenstadt (H)

Sendenhorst (NW)
Senftenberg (BR)
Siegburg (NW)
Siegen (NW)
Sigmaringen (BW)
Sindelfingen (BW)
Singen (BW)
Sinsheim (BW)
Sondershausen (T)
Sonneberg (T)
Bad Sooden (H)
Speyer (RP)
Sprendlingen (H)
Stade (NS)
Stadthagen (NS)
Stassfurt (SAA)
Stendal (SAA)
Stockach (BW)
Stockum (NW)
Straelen (NW)
Stralsund (MV)
Straubing (B)
Stuttgart (BW)
Suhl (T)
Sulz/Neckar (BW)
Tangermunde (SAA)
Telgte (NW)
Tittmoning (B)
Bad Tolz (B)
Torgau (SA)
Traunstein (B)
Treffurt (T)
Trier (RP)
Tübingen (BW)
Überlingen (BW)
Uelzen (NS)
Ulm (BW)
Ulrichstein (H)
Unna (NW)
Velbert (NW)
Verden/Aller (NS)
Viersen (NW)
Villingen (BW)

Vohburg/Donau (B)
Volklingen (S)
Wachtenheim (RP)
Waiblingen (BW)
Bad Waldsee (BW)
Waldheim (SA)
Waldshut (BW)
Wangen (BW)
Wanne-Eickel (NW)
Warendorf (NW)
Warstein (NW)
Wasserburg am Inn
  (B)
Wattenscheid (NW)
Weiden-Oberpfalz
  (B)
Weil am Rhein (BW)
Weilburg (H)
Weilheim (B)
Weimar (T)
Weingarten (BW)
Weinheim (BW)
Weismain (B)
Weissenburg (B)
Weissenfels (SAA)
Werl (NW)
Werne an der Lippe
  (NW)
Wernigerode (SAA)
Wertheim (BW)
Wesel (NW)
Wetzlar (H)
Wiesbaden (H)
Wilster (SH)
Bad Wimpfen (BW)
Bad Windsheim (B)
Winsen (S)
Wismar (MV)
Witten (NW)
Wolfach (BW)
Wolfenbüttel (NS)
Wolgast (MV)
Wolmirstedt (SAA)

Wormeln (NW)	Würzburg (B)	Zeulenroda (T)
Worms (RP)	Xanten (NW)	Zittau (SA)
Wülfrath (NW)	Zeitz (SAA)	Zweibrücken (RP)
Wünsiedel (B)	Zella-Mehlis (T)	Zwickau (SA)
Wuppertal (NW)	Zerbst (SAA)	

I do not claim that the above list is complete. It has been put together from a variety of sources, and there will be omissions, particularly of smaller places. Correspondence should be sent to the Direktor, Stadtarchiv, followed by the name of the city and the province or Länder.

In addition to the above, there are specialized archives in such places as Jena, for example, where you will find the archives of the Karl Zeiss Company and the Jena Glassworks. If you know your ancestor worked for a large corporation it may be worthwhile to write to the company concerned to ask if it has archival or personnel records available.

There is also the Red Cross Archives in Dresden (Das Zentral Verwaltungsarchiv des Deutschen Roten Kreuzes, Kaitzer Strasse, 01069 Dresden; phone: 011-49-35146780; fax: 011-49-3514678222; e-mail: info@drksachsen.de; website: www.drksachsen.de/). This may be useful if you are trying to trace someone who was a refugee from the area of Germany now in former Soviet territory.

Parish Archives (Pfarrarchiv)

Many of the city archives shown above also have local church records, but given below are separate church archives known to exist and *not* included in the major church archives previously listed. After the province code, a C or L is given in parentheses to indicate whether the archives hold Catholic or Lutheran records, or both.

Amöneburg (H) (C)	Essen (H) (C)
Balingen (BW) (L)	Flensburg (SH) (C)
Biberach (BW) (L and C)	Göttingen (NS) (L and C)
Bochum (NW) (L)	Gudow (SH) (L)
Bottrop (NW) (C)	Hagen (NW) (L and C)
Brakel (NW) (C)	Hattingen (NW) (L)
Burgsteinfurt (NW) (L and C)	Herford (NW) (L and C)
Duderstadt (NS) (L and C)	Herrenberg (BW) (L)
Duisburg (NW) (L)	Hof (B) (L)
Dulmen (NW) (L)	Höxter (NW) (C)
Emden (NS) (L)	Isny (BW) (L)
Emmerich (NW) (L and C)	Karlsruhe (BW) (L)
Engelskirchen (NW) (C)	Kassel (H) (L)
Erfurt (T) (L and C)	Kulmbach (B) (C)

Leer (H) (L)
Lich (H) (L)
Lübeck (SH) (L)
Methler (NW) (L)
Molzen (NS) (L)
Munstereifel (NW) (L)
Neuss (NW) (L)
Remagen (RP) (L and C)
Rottweil (BW) (C)
St. Goar (RP) (L)

Schwäbisch Hall (BW) (L)
Siegburg (NW) (C)
Stockum (NW) (C)
Überlingen (BW) (C)
Uelzen (NS) (L)
Viersen (NW) (C)
Wattenscheid (NW) (L and C)
Wetzlar (H) (L and C)
Xanten (NW) (C)
Zweibrücken (RP) (L)

Family Archives (Familienarchiv)

Many of the princely, noble, or prominent German families have either donated their family papers and records to the state or opened their documents to the general public. Searches can be made without charge, or by a fee, according to local decision. These family archives may be located in the original family residence (usually a Schloss, or castle) or in archives in the state, the city, or the village. You will have to do some letter-writing about this because the variations are infinite. If your ancestors were employed by these families, or were tenant farmers on the estate, the information can be of very great value to you.

The family archives I have been able to discover are listed below, showing the place, the abbreviation for the province or Länder, and the name of the family. (*Note*: The province codes are the same as those used above.)

Adelebsen (NS), Adelebsen
Ahausen (NW), Spee
Alme (NW), Spee zu Alme
Altenhof (SH), Reventlow
Althausen (BW), Württemberg
Amecke (NW), Wrede-Amecke
Amorbach (B), Leiningen
Anholt (NW), Salm
Antfeld (NW), Papen zu Antfeld
Apelern (NS), Münchhausen
Artelshofen (B), Harlach
Aschhausen (BW), Zeppelin
Assenheim (H), Solms-
 Rödelheim
Assumstadt (BW), Waldburg-
 Wolfegg
Aufsess (B), Aufsess

Augsburg (B), Fugger
Aulendorf (BW), Königsegg-
 Aulendorf
Banteln (NS), Benningsen
Beetzendorf (SAA), Von der
 Schulenburg
Beichlingen (T), Werthern-
 Beichlingen
Bentlage (NW), Wittgenstein-
 Berleburg
Berleburg (NW), Wittgenstein-
 Berleburg
Besselich (RP), Barton-Stedman
Bietigheim (BW), Hornstein
Binningen (BW), Hornstein
Birkenau (H), Unstadt
Birstein (H), Isenburg

Bödigheim (BW), Collenberg
Bodman (BW), Bodman
Boltzenburg (MV), Von Arnim
Haus Borg (NW), Kerkerinck
Braunfels (H), Solms-Braunfels
Breitenburg (SH), Rantzau
Breitenhaupt (NW), Kanne
Haus Brinke (NW), Korff-Bilkau
Buchholz (BW), Ow
Budingen (H), Ysenburg
Buldern (NW), Romberg
Burgsteinfurt (NW), Bentheim
Burkeim (BW), Fahnenberg
Caen (NW), Geyr
Calmsweiler (S), Buseck-Weber
Canstein (NW), Elverfeldt
Cappenberg (NW), Stein
Castell (B), Castell
Celle (NS), Lüneberg
Coesfeld (NW), Salm-Horstmar
Corvey (NW), Ratibor
Crassenstein (NW), Ansembourg
Crollage (NW), Ledebur
Dalwigksthal (H), Dalwigk
Darfeld (NW), Vischering
Derneburg (NS), Münster
Deutsch-Nienhof (SH),
   Hedemann-Heespen
Die Poltsdorf (B), Enderndorf
Diersburg (BW), Roeder
Diersfordt (NW), Wernigerode
Dillingen (B), Fuggers
Donaueschingen (BW),
   Fürstenberg
Donzdorf (BW), Rechberg
Drensteinfurt (NW), Landsberg-
   Velen
Dresden (SA), Wolkenstein
Bad Driburg (NW), Oeynhausen
Dulmen (NW), Croy
Durbach (BW), Windschläg
Dyck (NW), Reifferscheidt
Ebnet (BW), Gayling

Egelborg (NW), Oer
Eglofs (BW), Syrgenstein
Eichtersheim (BW), Venning
Elbenberg (H), Buttlar
Ellingen (B), Wrede
Eltville (H), Eltz
Erbach (H), Erbach
Erpernberg (NW), Wartenberg-
   Brenken
Erzeleben (SAA), Alvensleben
Eschenbach (B), Eschenbach
Essingen (BW), Woellwarth
Eybach (BW), Degenfeld-
   Schonburg
Fachsenfeld (BW), Fachsenfeld
Fischbach (B), Enderndorf
Frankenberg (B), Pöllnitz
Frankisch-Crumbach (H),
   Gemmingen
Furth-Burgfarrnbach (B), Pückler
Gärtringen (BW), Gärtringen
Gemünd (NW), Harff-Dreiborn
Gemünden (RP), Salis-Soglio
Gersfeld (H), Ebersberg-Froberg
Gödens (NS), Wedel
Göppingen (BW), Liebenstein
Gotha (T), Hohenlohe
Greifenberg (B), Perfall
Grevenburg (NW), Oeynhausen
Gross-Brunsrode (NS), Bülow
Grünsberg (B), Reichenbach
Guttenberg (B), Guttenberg
Burg-Guttenberg (BW),
   Gemmingen
Hahnstatten (RP), Bieberstein
Haidenburg (B), Aretin
Haimendorf (B), Rehlingen
Harff (NW), Mirbach
Havixbeck (NW), Twikkel
Heimerzheim (NW), Böselager
Heltorf (NW), Spee
Herbern (NW), Merveldt
Herdringen (NW), Fürstenberg

Heroldsberg (B), Geuder
Herrnstein (NW), Reichenstein
Hinnenburg (NW), Asseburg
Hohenstadt (BW), Adelmann
Höllinghofen (NW), Böselager
Hornberg (BW), Gemmingen
Hugstetten (BW), Mentzingen
Irmelshausen (B), Bibra
Jagsthausen (BW), Berlichingen
Jettingen-Eberstall (B),
  Stauffenberg
Kalbeck (NW), Vittinghoff
Kellenberg (NW), Hoensbroech
Kendenich (NW), Kempis
Kleinbottwar (BW), Schaubek
Königseggwald (BW), Aulendorf
Korschenbroich (NW),
  Wüllenweber
Kronburg (B), Westernach
Laibach (BW), Racknitz
Langenstein (BW), Douglas
Laubach (H), Solms-Laubach
Lauterbach (H), Riedesel
Lenthe (NS), Lenthe
Lich (H), Solms-Lich
Lipporg (NW), Galen
Loburg (NW), Elverfeldt
Marck (NW), Grüter
Marxwalde (BR), Hardenberg
Massenbach (BW), Massenbach
Merkstein (NW), Brauchitsch
Merlsheim (NW), Mühlen
Mespelbrunn (B), Ingelheim
Meuselwitz (SA), Seckendorff
Mitwitz (B), Würtzburg
Moyland (NW), Steengracht
Nassau (RP), Stein
Neuenburg (B), Gagern
Neuenstein (BW), Hohenlohe
Neunhof (B), Welser
Neuwied (RP), Wied
Niedenstein (BW), Venning

Niederstotzingen (BW), Malde-
  gem
Oberbalzheim (BW), Balzheim
Obernzenn (B), Seckendorff
Oberstadion (BW), Schönborn
Öhringen (BW), Hohenlohe
Ostwig (NW), Lüninck
Ottingen (B), Ottingen
Pöttmes (B), Gumppenberg
Rammersdorf (B), Eyb
Ratzenried (BW), Trauchberg
Regensburg (B), Thurn-Taxis
Rentweinsdorf (B), Rotenhan
Rheda-Wiedenbrück (NW),
  Tecklenburg
Rösberg (NW), Weichs
Rötha (SA), Friesen
Rugland (B), Crailsheim
Ruhr (NW), Mühlen
Rust (BW), Böcklinsau
Schatthausen (BW), Ravensburg
Schillingsfürst (B), Hohenlohe
Schlatt (BW), Reischach
Schlitz (H), Görtz
Schönstein (RP), Wildenburg
Schopfheim (BW), Roggenbach
Schwarmstedt (NS), Lenthe
Schwarzenberg (B),
  Schwarzenberg
Schwarzenraben (NW), Ketteler
Schweinsberg (H), Schweinsberg
Sigmaringen (BW), Hohenzollern
Simmelsdorf (B), Simmelsdorf
Singen (BW), Enzenberg
Somborn (H), Savigny
Stapel (NW), Raitz-Frentz-Droste
Steisslingen (BW), Stotzingen
Stetten (BW), Stetten
Sulzfeld (BW), Ravensburg
Surenberg (NW), Heereman-
  Zuydtwyck
Syburg (B), Geyern

Tambach (B), Ortenburg
Tannhausen (BW), Thannhausen
Tannheim (BW), Schaesberg
Thurnau (B), Giech
Trier (RP), Kesselstatt
Trockau (B), Trockau
Ullstadt (B), Frankenstein
Volkershausen (B), Stein-
    Ostheim
Vörden (NW), Haxthausen
Vornholz (NW), Nagel-Doornick
Waake (NS), Wangenheim
Waal (B), Leyen
Wachendorf (BW),
    Ow-Wachendorf
Wallerstein (B), Oettingen
Warthausen (BW), Warthausen

Weeze (NW), Loë
Weissenburg (B), Geyern
Welbergen (NW), Welbergen
Wernstein (B), Künsberg
Wertheim (BW), Löwenstein-
    Wertheim
Westerholt (NW), Westerholt
Westerwinkel (NW), Merveldt
Wewer (NW), Brenken
Wiesentheid (B), Wiesentheid
Wittgenstein (NW), Wittgenstein-
    Hohenstein
Wolfegg (BW), Waldburg-
    Wolfegg
Worms (RP), Hernsheim
Zeil (BW), Waldburg-Zeil

Libraries (Bibliotheken)

The public libraries in cities and towns should not be neglected as a source of information. They usually contain city directories, newspapers, and local histories, all of which may date back to the middle or early part of the nineteenth century. In many places, names have been abstracted from early newspapers and placed on index cards. Many libraries also contain details of local families if they have taken an active part in the affairs of the district.

Other Records

The LDS Church has some miscellaneous material on microfilm from Neubrandenburg, Rostock, and Schwerin. The Landeshauptarchiv in Dresden has eighty-four volumes of parish registers from former Sachsen Garnisonsorte (military posts in Saxony).

GENEALOGICAL ASSOCIATIONS IN GERMANY

There are a number of genealogical associations in Germany. Many are members of a national genealogical association: Deutsche Arbeitsge-meinschaft genealogischer Verbände e.V., known as the DAGV (Postfach 60 05 18, 63069 14405 Potsdam; e-mail: info@dagv.org; website: www. dagv.org/). I list these associations below. It is important that you make contact with the one operating in your area of Germany because (a) they will probably know if someone else has already researched your family; (b) many of them have their own libraries and archives, which may contain items of vital interest to you; (c) many of them publish magazines at regular intervals and will publish small ads or queries, either free or for a small charge. Some of them only accept queries for their own members, so you might consider joining.

The DAGV issues good advice in English to people sending inquiries to them, or to the individual associations. It is worthwhile giving you a précis of the advice.

1. There is no connection between the church records of the two major denominations. If you want a search made in a church archive or register, you must know the actual religion.

2. There can be no answer to questions about an ancestor unless you know a place of origin, birth, or marriage. Inquiries based on "Germany," or "Preussen," or "near Stuttgart" cannot be answered.

3. Do all the research you possibly can in your own country through family papers, wills, obituary notices, and family Bibles.

4. If you are asking questions about several people who came from different locations, write each query on a separate sheet of paper.

5. If you have already done some research, give all the details.

6. Good English is better than bad German. Use a computer, or print all names of persons and places.

7. Send *five* International Reply Coupons to cover postage and expenses. Donations are appreciated.

Bear in mind that addresses can change, and there can always be additions or deletions. Check the DAGV website at **www.dagv.org** for the most up-to-date information.

Arbeitsgemeinschaft für Familiengeschichte im Kulturkreis Siemens, Göbelstrasse 143-145, 13623 Berlin

Arbeitsgemeinschaft für mitteldeutsche Familienforschung, Berliner Strasse 31 a, 47533 Kleve; website: http://amf.genealogy.net

Arbeitsgemeinschaft für Saarländische Familienkunde, Hebbelstrasse 3, 66346 Püttlingen; website: www.saar-genealogie.de/

Arbeitsgemeinschaft Genealogie Magdeburg, Thiemstrasse 7, 39104 Magdeburg; website: http://ag-magdeburg.genealogy.net

Arbeitsgemeinschaft Genealogie Thüringen, Herderstrasse 35, 99096 Erfurt

Arbeitsgemeinschaft ostdeutscher Familienforscher; website: www. agoff.de/

Arbeitskreis donauschwäbischer Familienforscher, Goldmühlestrasse 30, 71065 Sindelfingen; website: http://akdff.genealogy.net

Arbeitskreis Familienforschung Osnabrück, Iburger Strasse 240, 49082 Osnabrück; website: www.osfa.de/

Arbeitskreis für Familienforschung im Hagener Heimatbund, Eilper Strasse 71, 58091 Hagen

Arbeitskreis für Siebenbürgische Landeskunde, Schloßstrasse 41, 74831 Gundelsheim; website: www.siebenbuergische-familienforschung.de/

Bayerischer Landesverein für Familienkunde, Ludwigstrasse 14/I – Zimmer 110, 80539 München; website: http://blf.genealogy.net

Bergischer Verein für Familienkunde, Gennebrecker Strasse 91, 42279 Wuppertal; website: www.bvff.de/

Brandenburgische Genealogische Gesellschaft "Roter Adler" e.V. , Postfach 60 03 13, 14403 Potsdam; website: www.bggroteradler.de/

Bund der Familienverbände, Rektoratsweg 123/25, 48159 Münster; website: www.familienverbaende-bdf.de/

Die Maus, Am Staatsarchiv 1/Fedelhören (Staatsarchiv), 28203 Bremen; website: http://maus.genealogy.net

Dresdner Verein für Genealogie e.V. , Postfach 192503, 01283 Dresden; website: www.dresden-genealogieverein.de/

Düsseldorfer Verein für Familienkunde, c/o Norbert Degenhard, Krummenweger Strasse 26, 40880 Ratingen; website: www.dvff.de.vu

Emsländische Landschaft, Arbeitskreis Familienforschung, Ludmillenstrasse 8, 49716 Meppen

Familienkundliche Arbeitsgemeinschaft der "Männer vom Morgenstern, Heimatbund an Elb- und Wesermündung", An der Packhalle V, Abt. 1, 27572 Bremerhaven; website: www.m-v-m.de/

Familienkundliche Gesellschaft für Nassau und Frankfurt , Mosbacher Strasse 55, 65187 Wiesbaden; website: http://fgnff.genealogy.net

Familienstiftung Pies-Archiv, Forschungszentrum Vorderhunsrück Altes Pfarrhaus, An der Kirche 1, D-56290 Dommershausen; website: www. piesverlag.de

Genealogische Gesellschaft Hamburg, Postfach 302042, 20307 Hamburg; website: http://gghh.genealogy.net

Genealogischer Kreis in der Freizeitgemeinschaft Siemens Erlangen, Freitzeitgemeinschaft Siemens, z. H. GK, Hartmannstrasse 17, 91052 Erlangen

Genealogischer Verein Chemnitz, Postfach 71 01 54, 09056 Chemnitz; website: www.gv-chemnitz.de/

Genealogisch-Heraldische Gesellschaft Göttingen, Postfach 2062, 37010 Göttingen; website: http://ghgg.genealogy.net

Gesellschaft für Familienforschung in der Oberpfalz, c/o Max Pöppl, Rachelstrasse 12, 93059 Regensburg; website: http://gfo.genealogy. net

Gesellschaft für Familienforschung in Franken, Archivstrasse 17 (Staatsarchiv), 90408 Nürnberg; website: www.gf-franken.de/

Gesellschaft für Familienkunde in Kurhessen und Waldeck, Postfach 10 13 46, 34013 Kassel; website: www.gfkw.de/

Gruppen Familien-und Wappenkunde in der Stiftung Bahn-Sozialwerk, Rauks Feld 5A, 44869 Bochum; website: http://gfw.genealogy.net

HEROLD, Archivstrasse 11, 14195 Berlin; website: www.herold-verein. de/

Hessische familiengeschichtliche Vereinigung, Karolinenplatz 3, 64289 Darmstadt; website: http://hfv.genealogy.net

Institut für Personengeschichte, Hauptstrasse 65, 64625 Bensheim; website: www.personengeschichte.de/

Landesarchiv Nordrhein-Westfalen Personenstandsarchiv Brühl, Schloßstrasse 10-12, 50321 Brühl; website: www.archive.nrw.de/

Leipziger Genealogische Gesellschaft, c/o Staatsarchiv Leipzig, Schongauerstrasse 1, 04328 Leipzig; e-mail: info@lgg-leipzig.de; website: www.lgg-leipzig.de/

Leps-Mielke-Stiftung, Neusser Wall 12, 50670 Köln

Niedersächsischer Landesverein für Familienkunde Am Bokemahle 14-16 (Stadtarchiv), 30171 Hannover; website: www.familienkunde-niedersachsen.de/

Oldenburgische Gesellschaft für Familienkunde, Marktplatz 6, 26209 Kirchhatten; website: www.familienkunde-oldenburg.de/

Pfälzisch-Rheinische Familienkunde, Rottstrasse 17, 67061 Ludwigshafen

Pommerscher Greif e.V. Verein für pommersche Familien-und Ortsgeschichte, Moosweg 37, 84326 Falkenberg; website: www.pommerscher-greif.de/

Roland zu Dortmund, Postfach 40 12, 58222 Schwerte; website: www. rolandgen.de/

Schleswig-Holsteinische Familienforschung, c/o Landesarchiv Schleswig-Holstein, Prinzenpalais, 24837 Schleswig; website: http://shfam.genealogy.net

Sippenverband Wallmichrath, c/o Klaus Wallmichrath, Schützenstrasse 9, 42553 Velbert

Stiftung Stoye, c/o Dr. Jochen Steinecke, Langenweddinger Strasse 8, 39122 Magdeburg

Upstalsboom-Gesellschaft für historische Personenforschung und Bevölkerungsgeschichte in Ostfriesland, Fischteichweg 16, 26603 Aurich; website: www.upstalsboom.org

Verband der Familien Lampe und verwandter Familien, Christoph Lampe, Simrockstrasse 28, 22587 Hamburg

Verein für Familienforschung e.V. Lübeck , Mühlentorplatz 2 (Mühlentorturm), 23552 Lübeck

Verein für Familienforschung in Ost- und Westpreußen, c/o Reinhard Wenzel, An der Leegde 23, D-29223 Celle; website: http://vffow.genealogy.net

Verein für Familien- und Wappenkunde in Württemberg und Baden, Postfach 105441, 70047 Stuttgart; website: http://vfwkwb.genealogy.net

Verein für Genealogie in Nordwürttemberg e.V., Ingersheimer Strasse 47, 71634 Ludwigsburg; website: www.genealogie-nordwuerttemberg.de/

Verein für mecklenburgische Familien- und Personengeschichte, c/o Prof. Dr. Hans-Dietrich Gronau, Fliederhof 2, 18107 Elmenhorst/Lichtenhagen; website: www.MFPeV.de/

Verein für Computergenealogie, c/o Klaus-Peter Wessel, Lampehof 58, 28259 Bremen; website: http://compgen.genealogy.net

Vereinigung für Familienkunde Elmshorn, Bi de Möhl 10b, 25336 Elmshorn

Vereinigung Sudetendeutscher Familienforscher, Stadt Regensburg, Amt für Archiv und Denkmalpflege, VSFF-SGA, Postfach 110643, 93019 Regensburg; website: http://www.vsff.de/

Werkgroep Genealogisch Onderzoek Duitsland , Herr Sekretariat: Herr Dr. W.R. Wybrands Marcussen, Rooseveltlaan 191, NL-1079 AP Amsterdam, Niederlande; website: http://www.wgod.nl

Westdeutsche Gesellschaft für Familienkunde, c/o Claus Geis, Unter Gottes Gnaden 34, 50859 Köln-Widdersdorf; website: http://wgff.genealogy.net

Zentralstelle für Personen- und Familiengeschichte, Volkmar Leonhard, An der Kreuzheck 15, 60529 Frankfurt/Main

There are also some organizations concerned with more specific subjects:

Anglo-German FHS, 14 River Reach, Teddington, London TW11 90L England; website: www.agfhs.org.uk/index.html

Mennonitischer Geschichtsverein, Am Hollerbrunnen 2A, 67295 Bolanden; website: www.mennoniten.de/geschichtsverein.html

Salzburger Verein e. V., Schleswiger Strasse 16, 33605 Bielefeld; website: http://salzburger.homepage.t-online.de/Verein.htm

The following organizations are sources of information about **Huguenotten (Huguenots)**:

Deutsche Hugenotten-Gesellschaft , Am Hafenplatz 9a, 34385 Bad Karlshafen; website: www.hugenotten.de/

Huguenot and Walloon Research Association, Malmaison, Church Street, Great Bedwyn, England SN8 3PE (information about Huguenot refugees from Germany)

Consistorium der Französischen Kirche, Joachim-Friedrich-Strasse 4, 10711 Berlin 31; website: www.franzoesische-kirche.de/

There are also hundreds of historical associations and societies in all the major cities and towns. It is impossible to list them all, but a search on the Internet should produce results. Historical organizations very often have a great deal of information about local families even if genealogy is not the main object of their existence.

CONTINUATION

This is usually the part of the book where the author melds together everything he has said in all previous pages and writes the magic word CONCLUSION. In a book about searching for your German roots (or any other roots) this cannot be written. Unless you are unbelievably lucky there will never be a conclusion, no end to the road, no finish to the story—there will always be gaps to be filled, questions to be answered. You may have traced your family back 500 years, but in one generation you may have a wife's first name but not her surname, in another you may have dates of baptisms and burials but no date (except an approximate one) for a marriage. These gaps will not mean your proven descent is incomplete, but they will bother you over the years, and you will keep on trying a new approach, thinking up a brilliant idea to solve the problem.

Anyway, do you really ever want to say FINISH? What would you do with your time then? If you started with your father's family, you can now try your mother's. You have grandparents to work on, and great-grandparents too. The possibilities are endless. You can even take on the mammoth project of tracing every living relative! I know one woman in New York who is doing just that—she can already produce over 300 cousins of various degrees, and she is still on the hunt for more!

Apart from the dull parade of "vital events" that make up your family tree, your search will bring you excitement and romance. You will have the thrill of the chase as, step-by-step, you go further back into history. You will have those magic moments when you open a long-awaited letter from Bavaria to find you have gone back another generation. You will find moments of intimacy in old letters and diaries. You may discover touching tributes to one of your ancestors—like one of my wife's Copland forebears who had these wonderful words inscribed on the tombstone of his parents:

> If all those who well knew and could record his integrity, public spirit, and benevolence, and her amiable manners and worth, had been im-

mortal, this memorial need not have been inscribed by their eldest son, William Copland of Colliston. A.D. 1808.

As you trace your family back you will want to know much more about the work they did, the clothes they wore, the houses they lived in, the area in which they were born. You can find all this in local history books, old newspapers, books on sociology, and so on. I found out many things about my sheep-farming ancestors. I know the breed they raised on the high fells above the ancestral valley of Swindale—Herdwicks; I know when they took their sheep to market in Kendal—every Wednesday; I know how much they got for their wool—8 shillings for 14 pounds in 1705; I know when they took the flocks up to the fells for the summer grazing—early in April; I know the food they ate, the clothes they wore, the furniture in their houses. These are the fascinating details that put thick foliage on the bare branches of the family tree.

During all the centuries the Baxters were raising their sheep and their children in their remote, lost dale, my wife's family—the Pearsons—were living some sixty miles away on the upper reaches of the River Tyne. Their life was very different from the Baxters'. Although they, too, had originally been hill farmers, they developed a nose for business and were soon owning lead mines and coal mines and ever-increasing estates. They were lords of the manors of Haltwhistle and Allendale and Hexham—totaling thousands of acres of good farmland and stone quarries and rich summer grazing. They married the daughters of the Earls of Derwentwater and played an active part in the fashionable life of London and Newcastle. They sent one son to manage lead mines in Scotland and another to fight in the lost cause of the Jacobite Rebellion of 1715.

You may discover many similar stories about your ancestors if you dig deep enough. If you are lucky you may well come into possession of family treasures you do not even know about now. As you make contact with distant relatives in the old country—a cousin in the Palatinate, another one in the Black Forest—you will eventually meet, make friendships, and who knows what family heirlooms will be passed on to you?

Perhaps you will find, as I once did, the ruins of an old house once built and occupied by an ancestor. I doubt, however, if any find could be more romantic than mine. Many years ago on a spring morning, just after daybreak, I was poking about in the ruins of an old house called Swindalehead. The silence was total, except for the sound of a few sheep grazing nearby. I found a massive beam that must have been the original support for the bedroom over the living room. Suddenly I noticed some faint carving in the wood. I rubbed away at the dirt and grime, and picked away at the indentation with an old squared nail I found.

Finally I could decipher it—JB ♂ IB 1539. I knew who they were! John Baxter and his wife, Isabel Wilkinson, and 1539 was the year of their marriage. I also know that in that year John was nineteen and his wife was eighteen, and they had been given the farm as a wedding present by John's father. Standing in the ruins in the silence and the stillness of that lonely, lovely valley of my ancestors, I could picture the two youngsters setting up house together—John carving the initials in the heavy beam, and Isabel holding firm the chair on which he stood. In that moment all my ancestors crowded around me and all my searching for my roots was worthwhile.

Go forward then—there is still magic in the world, and love and warmth and happiness.

GERMAN GENEALOGICAL ASSOCIATIONS IN NORTH AMERICA

Included here is a list of some of the German genealogical societies in North America. You can search on the Internet to see if there are any other societies in your area. I hope readers will realize that in many voluntary organizations addresses change with the change of officials, so you should check the society's website for the most current contact information.

THE UNITED STATES

American Historical Society of Germans from Russia
631 D Street, Lincoln, NE 68502-1199
Phone: 402-474-3363. Fax: 402-474-7229
E-mail: ahsgr@ahsgr.org
Website: www.ahsgr.org/

American/Schleswig-Holstein Heritage Society
PO Box 506, Walcott, IA 52773-0506
Phone: 563-284-4184. Fax: 563-284-4184
E-mail: ashhs@ashhs.org
Website: www.ashhs.org/

Berks County Genealogical Society
201 Washington Street, Reading, PA 19601
Phone: 610-921-4970
E-mail: berksgenes@dejazzd.com
Website: www.berksgenes.org/

Genealogical Society of Pennsylvania
1300 Locust Street (2nd floor), Philadelphia, PA 19107-5699
Phone: 215-545-0391. Fax: 215-545-0936
E-mail: ExecDir@GenPa.org
Website: www.genpa.org/

German-Bohemian Heritage Society
PO Box 822, New Ulm, MN 56073-0822
Website: www.rootsweb.com/~gbhs/index.html

Germanic Genealogy Societ
PO Box 16312, St. Paul, MN 55116-0312
E-mail: ggsqueries@hotmail.com
Website: www.rootsweb.com/~mnggs/GGS.html

German Research Association
PO Box 711600, San Diego, CA 92171-1600
E-mail: membership@gragen.org
Website: www.gragen.org/index.htm

Germans from Russia Heritage Society
1125 West Turnpike Avenue, Bismarck, ND 58501
Phone: 701-223-6167
E-mail: Rachel@grhs.org
Website: www.grhs.com/

Immigrant Genealogical Society
PO Box 7369, Burbank, CA 91510-7369
Phone: 818-848-3122; Fax: 818-716-6300
Website: www.immigrantgensoc.org/

Lancaster Mennonite Historical Society
2215 Millstream Road, Lancaster, PA 17602-1499
Phone: 717-393-9745. Fax: 717-393-8751
E-mail: lmhs@lmhs.org
Website: www.lmhs.org/

Mennonite Family History (magazine)
219 Mill Road, Morgantown, PA 19543-9701
Phone: 610-286-0258. Fax: 610-286-6860
E-mail: mast@masthof.com
Website: www.masthof.com/mfh.html

Mennonite Historians of Eastern Pennsylvania
PO Box 82, Harleysville, PA 19438-0082
Phone: 215-256-3020. Fax: 215-256-3023
E-mail: info@mhep.org
Website: www.mhep.org/

Mid-Atlantic Germanic Society
Membership: 2010 Bermondesey Drive, Mitchellville, MD 20721-4213
Website: www.magsgen.com/

Ostfriesen Genealogical Society of America
168 N. Lake Street, Forest Lake, MN 55025
E-mail: info@ogsa.us
Website: www.ogsa.us/

Palatines to America
611 East Weber Road, Columbus, OH 43211-1097
Phone: 614-267-4700
E-mail: membership@palam.org
Website: www.palam.org/
(There are also state chapters in Colorado, Illinois, Indiana, New
York, Ohio, Pennsylvania, West Virginia.)

Pommerscher Verein Freistadt
PO Box 204, Germantown, WI 53022-0204
E-mail: queries@pommerschervereinfreistadt.org
Website: http://pommerschervereinfreistadt.org/

Polish Genealogical Society of America
984 N. Milwaukee Avenue, Chicago, IL 60622
E-mail: PGSAmerica@aol.com
Website: www.pgsa.org/

Sacramento German Genealogy Society
PO Box 660061, Sacramento, CA 95866-0061
Website: www.sacgergensoc.org/

Schwenkfelder Library and Heritage Center
105 Seminary Street, Pennsburg, PA 18073
Phone: 215-679-3103. Fax: 215-679-8175
E-mail: info@schwenkfelder.com
Website: www.schwenkfelder.com/

South Central Pennsylvania Genealogical Society
PO Box 1824, York, PA 17405
E-mail: corsec@scpgs.org
Website: http://scpgs.org/

CANADA

Kitchener Public Library (Grace Schmidt Room)
85 Queen Street North, Kitchener, Ontario N2H 2H1
(This is also the address of the Waterloo-Wellington Branch of the
Ontario Genealogical Society.)
E-mail: watogs@yahoo.com
Website: www.waterlooogs.ca/

Society for German Genealogy in Eastern Europe
Box 905 Stn. M, Calgary, Alberta T2P 2J6
E-mail: membership@sggee.org
Website: www.sggee.org/

BIBLIOGRAPHY

Note: The Bibliography is a selective one of books I have found most useful in writing this book. It does not include others written in German, or the many books written about German settlement in states other than Maryland and Pennsylvania, or Canadian provinces other than Ontario and Nova Scotia. For these you should consult your local library or genealogical society.

Anderson, C., and E. Thode. *A Genealogist's Guide to Discovering Your Germanic Ancestors.* Cincinnati: 2000.

Baxter, A. *In Search of Your European Roots.* Third edition. Baltimore: 2001.

Bentz, E.M. *If I Can You Can Decipher Germanic Records.* San Diego: 1982.

Brandt, B., and E.R. Brandt. *Where to Look for Hard-to-find German-Speaking Ancestors in Eastern Europe.* Second edition. Baltimore: 1998.

Brandt, E. R., K. Cutkomp, M. Bellingham, K. E. Frye, and P. Lowe. *Germanic Genealogy: A Guide to Worldwide Sources and Migration Patterns.* Second edition. St. Paul, Minn., 1997.

DeMarce, V. *German Military Settlers in Canada.* Reisinger, WI: 1984.

Diffenderffer, F.R. *German Immigration into Pennsylvania. . . .* 1900. Reprint, Baltimore: 1988.

Egle, W.H. *Early Pennsylvania Land Records.* 1893. Reprint, Baltimore: 1997.

Eshleman, H.F. *Historic Background and Annals of the Swiss and German Pioneer Settlers of Southeastern Pennsylvania. . . .* 1917. Reprint, Baltimore 2000.

Faust, A.B., and G.M. Brumbaugh. *Lists of Swiss Emigrants in the Eighteenth Century to the American Colonies.* 2 vols. 1920–25. Reprint, Baltimore: 1991.

Genealogical Guide: German Ancestors from East Germany and Eastern Europe. Neustadt (Aisch), Germany: 1984.

Glazier, I.A., and P.W. Filby. *Germans to America: Lists of Passengers Arriving at U.S. Ports 1850–1897.* 67 vols. Wilmington, Del.: 1988–2001.

Hansen K.M. *Finding Your German Ancestors: A Beginner's Guide.* Provo, Utah: 1999.

Hansen, M.L. *The Atlantic Migration, 1607–1860.* Cambridge, Mass.: 1940.

Henning and Ribbe, *Handbuch des Genealogie.* Neustadt, Germany: 1972.

Hocker, E.W. *Genealogical Data Relating to the German Settlers of Pennsylvania and Adjacent Territory.* Baltimore: 1989.

Irish, D.R. *Pennsylvania German Marriages.* 1982. Reprint, Baltimore: 1999.

Jensen, L.D. *Genealogical Handbook of German Research.* Pleasant Grove, Utah: 1980.

Jones, G. *German-American Names.* Third edition. Baltimore: 2006.

Jones, H.Z, Jr. *Even More Palatine Families.* 3 vols. Camden, Maine: 2002.

Jones, H.Z, Jr. *More Palatine Families.* Universal City, Calif.: 1991.

Jones, H.Z, Jr. *The Palatine Families of Ireland,* Second edition. Camden, Maine: 1990.

Jones, H.Z, Jr. *The Palatine Families of New York 1710.* 2 vols. Universal City, Calif.: 1985.

Kessler, G. *Die Familiennamen der Juden in Deutschland.* Jerusalem: 1935.

Knittle, W.A. *Early Eighteenth Century Palatine Emigration.* 1937. Reprint, Baltimore: 1997.

MacWethy, L.D. *The Book of Names Especially Relating to the Early Palatines and the First Settlers in the Mohawk Valley.* 1933. Reprint, Baltimore: 1999.

Meynen, E. *Bibliography on the Colonial Germans of North America* (originally published as *Bibliography on German Settlements in Colonial North America*). Leipzig, Germany, 1937. Reprint, Baltimore: 1982.

Minerva Handbücher. *Archiv in Deutschsprachigen Raum.* Berlin: 1974.

Moltman, G. *Germans to America: 300 Years of Immigration 1683–1983,* Stuttgart, Germany: 1982.

Nead, D.W. *The Pennsylvania-German in the Settlement of Maryland.* 1914. Reprint, Baltimore: 1975.

Newman, H.W. *The Flowering of the Maryland Palatinate.* 1961. Reprint, Baltimore: 1998.

Otterness, Philip. *Becoming German: The 1709 Palatine Migration to New York.* Ithaca, N.Y.: 2007.

Pennsylvania German Society. *Pennsylvania German Church Records.* 3 vols. Baltimore: 1983

_____. *Pennsylvania German Fraktur.* Breinigsville, Pa.: 1983. Examples of German script.

Rupp, I.D. *A Collection of Upwards of Thirty Thousand Names of German . . . Immigrants in Pennsylvania from 1727 to 1776.* 1876. Reprint, Baltimore: 2000.

Schenk, T., R. Froelke, and I. Bork. *The Wuerttemberg Emigration Index.* 7 vols. Salt Lake City: 1986–.

Simmendinger, U. *True and Authentic Register of Persons . . . Who in the Year 1709 . . . Journeyed from Germany to America.* 1934. Reprint, Baltimore: 1991.

Smith, C.N., and A. Smith. *Encyclopedia of German-American Genealogical Research.* New York: 1976.

Staudt, R.W. *Palatine Church Visitations, 1609, Deanery of Kusel.* 1930. Reprint, Baltimore: 1998.

Steigerwald, J. *Tracing Romania's German Minority* (Danubian Swabians). Winona, Minn.: 1985.

Stoever, J.C. *Early Lutheran Baptisms and Marriages in Southeastern Pennsylvania* (originally published as *Records of Rev. John Casper Stoever*). 1896. Reprint, Baltimore: 1998.

Strassburger, R.B. and W.J. Hinke. *Pennsylvania German Pioneers: A Publication of the Original Lists of Arrivals in the Port of Philadelphia from 1727 to 1808.* 3 vols. 1934. Reprint, Baltimore: 1992.

Tepper, M. *American Passenger Arrival Records: A Guide to the Records of Immigrants Arriving at American Ports by Sail and Steam.* Updated and enlarged. 1993. Reprint, Baltimore: 1999.

_____. *Emigrants to Pennsylvania, 1641–1819 . . . from the Pennsylvania Magazine of History and Biography.* Baltimore, 1975. Reprint, Baltimore: 1999.

_____. *Passenger Arrivals at the Port of Baltimore, 1820–1834.* 1982. Reprint, Baltimore: 1999.

_____. *Passenger Arrivals at the Port of Philadelphia, 1800–1819.* Baltimore: 1986.

Thode, Ernest. *Address Book for Germanic Genealogy.* Sixth edition. Baltimore: 1997.

Thode, Ernest. *German-English Genealogical Dictionary.* Baltimore: 1992.

Wright, R.S. III. *Ancestors in German Archives.* Baltimore: 2004.

Wright, R.S. III, N.S. Rives, M.J. Kirkham, S.S. Bunting. *Meyers Orts- und Verkehrs-Lexikon des Deutschen Reichs. With Researcher's Guide and Translations of the Introduction, Instruction for the Use of the Gazetteer, and Abbreviations.* In Three Volumes. Baltimore: 2000.

Yoder, D. *Pennsylvania German Immigrants, 1709–1786.* 1980. Reprint, Baltimore: 1998.

———. *Rhineland Emigrants.* Baltimore: 1998.

Zimmerman, G.J. and M. Wolfert. *German Immigrants: Lists of Passengers Bound from Bremen to New York (1847–1867).* 3 vols. Baltimore, 1985–88. 4th vol. *(1868–1871)* by M. Wolfert. Baltimore: 1993.

Canada

Baxter, A. *In Search of Your Roots.* Toronto: 1978, 1991.

———. *In Search of Your Canadian Roots.* 3rd edition. 1994. Reprint, Baltimore: 2000.

Bell, W.P. *The Foreign Protestants and the Settlement of Nova Scotia.* Toronto: 1961.

DesBrisay, M.B. *History of Lunenburg County.* Halifax: 1870.

Eby, E. *A Biographical History of Early Settlers and Their Descendants in Waterloo Township.* 1895. Reprint, Kitchener, Ontario: 1971.

Fretz, J.W. *People Apart.* St. Jacobs, Ontario: 1971.

Johnson, R. *150 Years First Mennonite Church* [Kitchener]. Kitchener, Ontario: 1963.

Leibbrandt, G. *Little Paradise* [Waterloo County, 1800–1937]. Kitchener, Ontario: 1980.

Moyer, W.G. *This Unique Heritage* [Waterloo County]. Kitchener, Ontario: 1971.

Punch, T. *Genealogical Research in Nova Scotia.* Halifax: 1978.

Reaman, G.E. *The Trail of the Black Walnut* [Pennsylvania to Canada]. 1965. Reprint, Baltimore: 1993.

Uttley, W.V. *A History of Kitchener* [1865–1944]. 1937. Reprint, Kitchener, Ontario: 1975.

Note: Three early German newspapers (*Canada Museum, Deutsche Canadier,* and *Berliner Journal*) have been indexed for birth, marriage, and death entries by the Kitchener Public Library.

INDEX